Rethinking America 3

★★★★★★★★★★★★★★★★★★★★★★★★★★★★★★★★★★★★★★★

An Advanced Cultural Reader

Second Edition

M. E. Sokolik
University of California, Berkeley

HH HEINLE & HEINLE PUBLISHERS

I(T)P™ *an International Thomson Publishing Company*

Boston – Albany – Bonn – Cincinnati – Detroit – London – Madrid –
Melbourne – Mexico City – New York – Pacific Grove – Paris –
San Francisco – Tokyo – Toronto – Washington

The publication of *Rethinking America 3, An Advanced Cultural Reader* was directed by members of the Newbury House ESL/EFL Team at Heinle & Heinle Publishers:

Erik Gundersen: Senior Editor, ESL/ELT
Charlotte Sturdy: Market Development Director
Mike Burggren: Production Services Coordinator
Stanley J. Galek: Vice President and Publisher

Also participating in the publication of this program were:
Managing Developmental Editor: Amy Lawler
Developmental Editor: John Chapman
Assistant Editor: Jill Kinkade
Manufacturing Coordinator: Mary Beth Hennebury
Project Manager/Interior Designer: Linda Dana Willis
Cover Designer: Gina Petti
Cover Artist: Roy Lichtenstein
Compositor: Modern Graphics, Inc.
For permission to use copyrighted material, grateful acknowledgment is made to the copyright holders on the Credits page, which are hereby made part of this copyright page.

ISBN: 0-8384-4732-5

Front cover illustration: Girl with Hair Ribbon by Roy Lichtenstein, © Estate of Roy Lichtenstein

ACKNOWLEDGMENTS

★★

The fact that only my name appears on the cover seems a misrepresentation. Many, many people have helped in putting these volumes together. First and foremost, I would like to thank my Developmental Editor, John Chapman. His clarity of vision, insightful ideas, and masterful organization made this process much smoother than it otherwise would have been. Second, I would like to thank Erik Gundersen, Senior Editor, Heinle & Heinle for his unstinting support of the series and its expansion. I would also like to express my appreciation to Amy Lawler, Managing Developmental Editor, for doing such a great job in pulling all the pieces together and making sure everything was done right.

Other people at Heinle & Heinle have made valuable contributions as well. Joyce LaTulippe, Associate Developmental Editor, and Jonathan Boggs, Marketing Development Director, helped with the initial conception and development of the series. Jill Kinkade, Assistant Editor and Anne Sokolsky, Permissions Editor, dealt with the near-impossible task of getting rights to the authentic selections. And Becky Stovall, CNN Executive Producer in Atlanta, tracked down all the CNN video clips used in the series.

I also want to thank the reviewers and focus-group participants, whose insights and suggestions aided in the revision of the original text and in the conception of the two new volumes in the series:

Leslie Adams, Santa Ana College, CA

Alicia Aguirre, Cañada College, CA

Thom Allen, Chabot College, CA

Angelina Arellanes-Núñez, El Paso Community College, TX

Mardelle Azimi, California State University at Fullerton, CA

Victoria Badalamenti, LaGuardia Community College, NY

Gerald Lee Boyd, Northern Virginia Community College, VA

Pam Breyer, Braille Institute, CA

Mary Lou Byrne, Triton College, IL

Judi Camacho, Harper College, IL

Karen Carlson, Contra Costa College, CA

Jennifer Castello, Cañada College, CA

Anne Dorobis, Language Training Institute, NJ

Kathleen Flynn, Glendale Community College, CA

Ellen Clegg, ELS Language Center, CA

Patty Heiser, University of Washington Extension, WA

Jan Herwitz, ELS Language Center, San Francisco, CA

Gregory Keech, City College of San Francisco, CA

Julie Kim, University of Pennsylvania, PA

Tay Leslie, ELS Language Center, Los Angeles, CA

Kathleen Letellier, University of California Berkeley Extension, CA

Emily Lites, American Business English, CO

Robyn Mann, Harper College, IL

Roxanne Nuhaily, University of California, San Diego Extension, CA

Judith L. Paiva, Northern Virginia Community College, VA

Anita Razin, Santa Ana College, CA

Jan Rinaldi, Rio Hondo College, CA

Sandy Saldana, Triton College, IL

Irene Schoenberg, Hunter College, NY

Jane Selden, LaGuardia Community College, NY

Kathy Van Ormer, EDTP UAW-Ford National Programs Center, IL

Rose White, Lindsay Hopkins Technical Education Center, FL

James Wilson, Mount San Antonio College, CA

Finally, I want to thank every student who has ever said to me, "I don't understand." That statement alone has prompted me to try to put into writing answers to important questions. I hope I have succeeded.

—M. E. Sokolik

iii

DEDICATION

To Jim Duber

CONTENTS

★★★

PREFACE

★★★

Rethinking America is a multi-skill cultural series for students of English as a Second Language. Each book has ten broad topic areas. However, the subject matter in these areas varies from book to book. *Rethinking America* incorporates *authentic texts* as a source of reading. Authentic texts give the student an entry into understanding American culture by hearing authentic voices writing about their views and experiences. These readings also represent a variety of genres: newspaper articles and essays, poems, short stories, charts, graphs, and many others.

The readings and activities throughout *Rethinking America* foster cultural awareness, understanding, and interaction among students, and between students and their local setting, whether they are studying English in the U.S. or in another country. This series is intended to get students to examine not only American cultural values, but their own cultural values as well. Through these readings and activities, students engage in meaningful dialogues, and in the process, refine their English language skills.

Many of the changes and additions in this new edition stem from the thoughtful suggestions of students and teachers who have used *Rethinking America* over the years and from the suggestions of reviewers who carefully examined all three new manuscripts as we developed the series. It was extremely gratifying to be able to make use of these ideas as we expanded the original book into a three-book series.

This expansion involved several different types of changes. First of all, there are two new books at the intermediate and high-intermediate levels. Secondly, we have increased the scope of the reading comprehension sections, added specific reading strategies instruction in each chapter, and provided some exciting new ancillary components, including a video segment to accompany each chapter and an Almanac containing supplementary information at the back of each book. Thirdly, all follow-up activities now include exercises which are relevant to students who are using the book in a setting outside of the United States as well as within the U.S.

ORGANIZATION

Chapter Organization Each chapter is organized around a central theme and divided into two subthemes.

Each subtheme contains two readings that examine the topic from different points of view.

INTRODUCTORY MATERIALS

Before You Read Each reading is introduced by a photo, chart, or some other visual opener related to the reading topic. A brief preview of the reading follows, and students are encouraged to think about what they already know about the topic and to answer some questions about the preview.

Cultural Cues Information that may be culture-specific, such as references to television shows or historical figures, is explained before the reading.

About the Author Brief biographies of many of the authors are included. Photos of major figures in American culture are also provided.

THE READING

Each reading includes line numbers for easy reference by the student and teacher. In addition, some words are highlighted for quick reference.

Within each chapter, a video segment related to the topic and obtained from the CNN video archives is listed. Each video clip is accompanied by a set of suggested discussion questions.

EXPANSION MATERIALS

Check Your Comprehension Following each reading are five or more questions regarding the content of the reading.

Reading Strategy A specific reading strategy is highlighted in each follow-up reading activity. A brief statement about the strategy appears in a box in the margin along with a reference to the Reading Strategy Guide in the front of the book which contains a more complete explanation of the strategy.

Vocabulary In this section, students work with the vocabulary from the reading. The activities are varied and designed to keep the interest level high: some ask the students to think about the grammatical context of vocabulary, such as the use of prepositions in idiomatic phrases; some are matching and fill in the blank exercises; still others are games, such as word searches or crossword puzzles.

Think About It This section asks students to go beyond the factual content of a reading and relate their own knowledge and experience to the themes that are introduced. These questions sometimes ask students to apply their understanding to projects, such as participating in simulations, or looking at outside materials such as magazines and newspapers.

Synthesis At the end of each chapter, a section of exercises and activities helps students integrate the ideas presented in the four readings of each chapter. These activities are designed to be relevant to students inside as well as outside the U.S.

Discussion and Debate This section presents several questions that can be used for class discussion or debate. This activity encourages students to come up with their own questions, as well.

Writing Topics The writing topics present different levels of writing tasks, from simple question-and-answer assignments or single-paragraph writing, to journal entries and short essays.

On Your Own This section suggests projects that can be done outside of class. These activities include watching videos, conducting surveys, doing library or Internet

research, as well as an array of other student-centered pursuits.

BONUS FEATURES

CNN Video Segments Each volume of the *Rethinking America* series has an accompanying CNN video. The clips on this video are closely tied to one or more of the readings in the *Rethinking America* text. Questions are included in the text to foster discussion of the video. The video transcriptions are available and appear in the Instructor's Manual.

The Almanac An almanac filled with stimulating and rich cultural information is found at the back of each book. It includes a list of major events in U.S. history, maps, temperature conversion tables, and other general information.

Instructor's Manual An Instructor's Manual is available to help make best use of the features of *Rethinking America*. This Manual includes not only answer keys, but also tips for using the video segments, related Internet and other outside information, and guidelines for using the series in EFL settings. The transcriptions for the CNN video also appear in the Instructor's Manual.

Reference Guide to Reading Strategies

★★★

Strategies

The following reading strategies are introduced and practiced in *Rethinking America*:

Active Reading   Reading actively means creating questions and comments about a text as you read it. This can help you understand and remember ideas and information. As you read, write questions and comments in the margin of your reading.

Finding and Understanding the Main Idea   The main idea is the central, most important idea in the reading. Finding and understanding the main idea will help you understand the central purpose of the reading.

Identifying Topic Sentences   A topic sentence states the main idea of the reading. Finding the topic sentence will help you understand the key message of the reading.

Making Inferences   Inferences are conclusions you make from information available to you. Sometimes readings contain suggestions rather than direct statements. When this happens, you have to guess, or make an inference about the message or purpose of the reading.

Reading Aloud   Reading Aloud simply means speaking what you are reading, rather than reading silently. When you read aloud you hear the sound of words and phrases. Reading aloud can help you understand new words and information.

Scanning   Scanning means reading quickly, without reading every word, in order to *find specific information* in a reading.

Skimming   Skimming means reading quickly, without reading every word, in order to *get the main idea* of a reading. When you skim, look at titles, illustrations and anything else in a reading that will quickly give you information.

Summarizing   Summarizing means taking only the most important ideas and information from a reading and putting them in your own words. Try fitting your summaries on index cards.

Understanding Arguments   To understand an argument made by an author, you must identify what the author wants to convince you of, and find the ideas the author uses to support this argument.

Understanding by Categorizing   Categorizing means placing information into groups or categories. Putting ideas into two or more different categories can help you get a better understanding of the relationships between ideas in a reading.

Understanding Contrasts   Contrasting means comparing two things to see the differences between them. You can use two different color highlighters to mark contrasting ideas in a text.

Understanding Definitions   Definitions are the meanings of words. Often, the definition of an unfamiliar word can be found in the reading itself. You can learn the meaning of a difficult word by looking at how the word is used in the sentence or surrounding sentences.

Understanding Descriptions   Descriptions are explanations of what something is like. Good descriptions help the reader to get a strong picture of what is being described.

Understanding Dialect   A dialect is a form of a language spoken in one part of a country which is different from the standard official language. Readings sometimes include dialects to give the reader a feel for the sound of the language in certain regions of the country.

Understanding Humor   Sometimes it can be difficult to understand the humor of another language and culture. However, by looking out for areas where the author exaggerates, or writes something which is clearly the opposite of what is true (sarcasm), you can often spot areas of humor in a reading.

Understanding Intention   Understanding intention means understanding the *reason* the author wrote the piece.

Understanding Long Sentences   When trying to understand a long sentence, it helps to break the sentence down into smaller parts.

Understanding Point of View   The same situation can be looked at differently by different people. A point of view is the way one person sees a situation. Sometimes the author is not the only one with a clear point of view—the characters or people quoted within the text can also have their own points of view.

Understanding Processes   A process is a sequence of related events. Understanding the process of events in a reading helps you see the order in which events happen. Look for words like "first," "second," "then," "next," and "finally" to help you understand a process.

Understanding Through Outlining   An outline is a numbered, structured grouping of the main points of a reading. Creating an outline helps you understand the structure of a reading by giving you a simplified picture of these main points.

★★★

The American Dream

What is the "American Dream"? Is it different from the dreams of other nations? In this chapter, you will read about two ideas associated with the American Dream: immigration and housing. How are these ideas related to the American Dream?

PART ONE

A NATION OF IMMIGRANTS

The United States is known as a "nation of immigrants." Throughout the centuries,
the United States has welcomed people from many countries to its shores.
Just as immigration continues today, so does the controversy surrounding it.

Before You Read

Arriving at Ellis Island

The following reading first discusses Ellis Island, a part of New York City
and New Jersey, which was the main point of entry into the United States
for millions of immigrants during the nineteenth and early twentieth centuries. Then, it tells the story of one Italian immigrant who passed through
Ellis Island.

Before you read, think about the following questions:

• What are your country's immigration policies?
• What do you think might be the advantages and disadvantages of a
  "nation of immigrants"?

Cultural Cues	
	Emma Lazarus An American poet and essayist who was born in New York City in 1849 and died in 1887; she is best known as the writer of the poem, "The New Colossus," which is inscribed on the Statue of Liberty.
	P.S. 22 in Queens Public School Number 22 in Queens, one of the five boroughs of New York City.
	Prohibition The period from 1920 to 1933 during which it was illegal to produce or drink any alcoholic beverages in the United States.

About the Author	
	Dinitia Smith has written for many magazines and newspapers, including the *New York Times*. She is the author of the novel *The Illusionist*, published in 1997.

READING

Find out more about **scanning** by looking in the Reference Guide to Reading Strategies on pages xii–xiv.

Scanning

Scanning means reading quickly while looking for specific information. Scan this article and complete the table below. Then, answer the question that follows it.

Date	Event
1892–1924	
April 17, 1907	
	75% of white immigrants were indentured servants
	one-third of immigrants returned home
by the year 2000	

Review the facts and dates you put in the table. Why do you think the author included them in the article?

Now, read the article more carefully.

ELLIS ISLAND

by Dinitia Smith

For many Americans, Ellis Island is a holy ground, the entry point for the ancestors of more than 100 million people, 40 percent of the country's population. From 1892 to 1924, more than 12 million people entered the United States through Ellis Island. On one day (April 17, 1907) 11,747 immi-
5 grants were processed there.

In a nation of well over a hundred ethnic groups, Ellis Island is the setting of America's one great unifying epic. While other countries have their own national legends, France has its Chanson de Roland, Spain its El Cid—America has the myth of the Golden Door, through which the "huddled
10 masses yearning to breathe free," as Emma Lazarus puts it, stepped and found freedom and prosperity at last. Paradoxically, that myth is being rethought and rewritten just as the museum at Ellis Island—started in a burst of patriotic nostalgia—is about to be dedicated.

The image of the immigrant as poor, oppressed, and uprooted is giving
15 way under the weight of new scholarship. Most people who came to the New World during the peak immigration years had at least the means to pay for the journey, and the stamina and health to withstand it. They came seeking better jobs more often than freedom. (Of course, many didn't find freedom at all. Not only were blacks imported as slaves, but before 1780,
20 75 percent of all white immigrants who settled south of New England were indentured servants.) For the most part, the people who came willingly brought the structures of their old cultures with them and used their traditions to build lives there. Perhaps most startling of all, it has recently been shown that a third of all those who had come to America during the twentieth
25 century have chosen to go home again—10 million out of 30 million people.

New York, meanwhile, is once again becoming a city of émigrés. More and more foreign-born people are settling here. By the year 2000, 56 percent of New York City's population will be immigrants and their children. Dominicans are currently the biggest group, followed by Jamaicans and Chinese.
30 At P.S. 22 in Queens, the students speak twenty languages. And in the New York City courts these days, there is a frequent demand for interpreters who know Wolof, a language spoken in West Africa and in New York by Senegalese street merchants.

The new immigrants have reversed the city's declining population and
35 are stemming the decrease in the labor force. They are revitalizing dying-neighborhoods, setting up shop in empty stores on Flatbush Avenue, bringing the infinite variety of their cultures to the great mix that is the city.

A New Blueprint

Even today, Guerino Salerni remembers the touch of his grandfather
40 Luigi's whiskers as he kissed him goodbye. When Salerni, now 84, talks
about leaving for America in 1919—when he was 14—tears still come to
his eyes. "It was the last time I saw him," says Salerni. "He was quite a
fellow." Guerino Salerni came from a family of stonemasons in a medieval
hill town in the region of Abruzzi, east of Rome. As a boy, Salerni could
45 build a home of stones in the fields and it would stand.

Salerni's father had first come to the United States in 1896. He found
work in construction, traveling back and forth between the U.S. and Italy
regularly, each time begetting a child. In 1918, Salerni's father decided it
was time for the rest of the family to come. Like many immigrants, they
50 traveled with a group from their village. There was Salerni's stepmother
(his mother had died), his sister, and a dozen ladies whose husbands had
already journeyed ahead.

Salerni hadn't seen his father in five years, but as the ship docked near
Ellis Island, he spotted him down below in a motorboat. "Where's Mama?
55 Where's Mama?" his father cried. Salerni's stepmother threw down a bottle
of Centerba, a liqueur from Abruzzi, in greeting—even though America was
in the midst of Prohibition.

Because there had been a death from typhoid fever aboard the ship,
Salerni spent ten days in quarantine before he was reunited with his father
60 for good. When he grew up, Salerni became an architect, working on a
number of projects in New York City—including the construction of East
River Drive—continuing the traditions of his Italian ancestors.

Source: *New York Magazine*

Check Your Comprehension

1. What is meant by the "myth of the Golden Door"?

2. According to the author, what were the real circumstances and motives of the immigrant in the early part of the twentieth century?

3. What benefits does the author see immigrants bringing to New York?

4. What is the Salerni family tradition? How far does it go back?

VOCABULARY Using Prepositions

Read the following sentences and write the correct preposition in the blanks.

1. _____ many Americans, Ellis Island was the entry point _____ the ancestors _____ more than 100 million people.

2. _____ April 17, 1907, 11,747 immigrants were processed _____ Ellis Island.

3. Many immigrants came _____ "the Golden Door" and found freedom and prosperity _____ last.

4. Most people who came _____ the New World during the peak immigration years had _____ least the means _____ pay _____ the journey.

5. _____ 1780, 75 percent _____ all white immigrants who settled south _____ New England were indentured servants.

6. A third _____ all those who came _____ America chose _____ go home again—10 million _____ _____ 30 million people.

7. _____ the year 2000, 56 percent of New York City's population will be immigrants and their children.

8. Dominicans are currently the biggest group, followed _____ Jamaicans and Chinese.

9. The new immigrants are slowing the decrease _____ the labor force.

10. They are setting _____ shop in empty stores _____ Flatbush Avenue.

THINK ABOUT IT

 Watch the CNN video on immigrants in New York City.
Discuss these questions:

1. How have immigration trends in New York City changed?

2. Why does the 1990 immigration law do?

3. According to the video, why do people immigrate to the U.S.?

1. If you've ever been to Ellis Island, what did you think of it? If you haven't been to Ellis Island, would you like to visit it? Why?

2. The words inscribed on the Statue of Liberty are taken from a poem written in 1883 by Emma Lazarus, part of which is given below:

> *The New Colossus*
> Give me your tired, your poor,
> Your huddled masses yearning to breathe free,
> The wretched refuse of your teeming shore,
> Send these, the homeless, tempest-tost, to me,
> I lift my lamp beside the golden door!

Look up any words in this poem you don't understand, and rewrite it in your own language. Then answer the following questions:

  a. What is the relationship between this poem and the article by Denita Smith?

b. What do you think about this poem and the ideas expressed by it?

c. The Salerni family had a long history of working in the construction business. Does your family have a history in a particular profession? List all the professions in your family that you know about. Do you see any patterns? Discuss your family's history with your classmates.

Before You Read

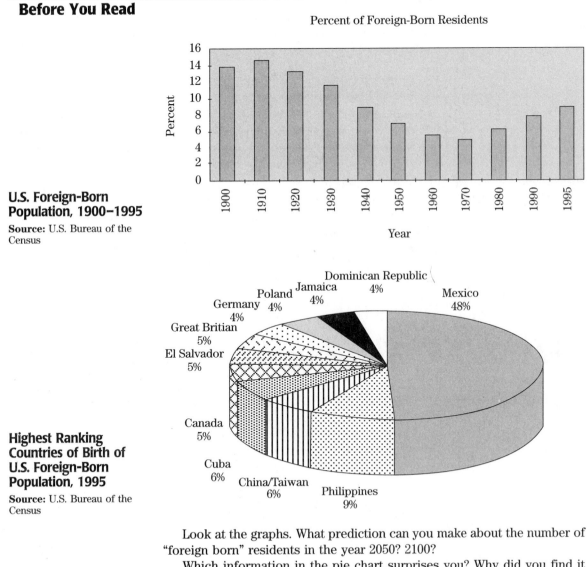

Percent of Foreign-Born Residents

U.S. Foreign-Born Population, 1900–1995

Source: U.S. Bureau of the Census

Highest Ranking Countries of Birth of U.S. Foreign-Born Population, 1995

Source: U.S. Bureau of the Census

Look at the graphs. What prediction can you make about the number of "foreign born" residents in the year 2050? 2100?

Which information in the pie chart surprises you? Why did you find it surprising?

In the following reading the author examines multiculturalism in the United States.

Before you read, think about the following questions:

- How do you define *multicultural*?
- What are the advantages of a multicultural society? What are the disadvantages?

Cultural Cues

Lower East Side A racially diverse neighborhood in Manhattan, which provided a first home in the United States for a wide range of immigrant groups over the past 150 years; early residents were mostly Italian, Eastern European and Russian Jews, Ukrainians, Greeks, and Poles. Current residents include people from China, Central and South America, Puerto Rico, and India.

Memorial Day A holiday on the last Monday in May, honoring those who died in war; it marks the unofficial beginning of summer in the United States and is celebrated with picnics and barbecues.

About the Author

Ishmael Reed was born in 1938 in Buffalo, New York. He now lives in Oakland, California. He has taught at Yale, Harvard, and Dartmouth universities. He now teaches at the University of California, Berkeley. He has written several books—novels and collections of essays. These books include *Mumbo Jumbo*, *Reckless Eyeballing*, and *Writin' is Fightin'*, from which this excerpt is taken.

AMERICA: The Multicultural Society

by Ishmael Reed

At the annual Lower East Side Jewish Festival yesterday, a Chinese woman ate a pizza slice in front of Ty Thuan Duc's Vietnamese grocery store. Beside her a Spanish-speaking family patronized a cart
5 *with two signs: "Italian Ices" and "Kosher by Rabbi Alper." And after the pastrami ran out, everybody ate knishes.*

—*New York Times*, June 23, 1983

On the day before Memorial Day 1983, a poet called me to describe a
10 city he had just visited. He said that one section included mosques, built by the Islamic people who dwelled there. Attending his reading, he said,

were large numbers of Hispanic people, forty thousand of whom lived in the same city. He was not talking about a fabled city located in some mysterious region of the world. The city he'd visited was Detroit.

15   A few months before, as I was leaving Houston, Texas, I heard it announced on the radio that Texas's largest minority was Mexican-American, and though a foundation recently issued a report critical of bilingual education, the taped voice used to guide the passengers on the air trams connecting terminals in Dallas Airport is in both Spanish and English. If the trend

20 continues, a day will come when it will be difficult to travel through some sections of the country without hearing commands in both English and Spanish; after all, for some western states, Spanish was the first written language and the Spanish style lives on in the western way of life.

    Such blurring of cultural styles occurs in everyday life in the United

25 States to a greater extent than anyone can imagine and is probably more prevalent than the sensational conflict between people of different backgrounds that is played up and often encouraged by the media. The result is what the Yale professor, Robert Thompson, referred to as a cultural bouillabaisse, yet members of the nation's present educational and cultural

30 elect still cling to the notion that the United States belongs to some vaguely defined entity they refer to as "Western civilization," by which they mean, presumably, a civilization created by the people of Europe, as if Europe can be viewed in monolithic terms. Is Beethoven's Ninth Symphony, which includes Turkish marches, a part of Western civilization, or the late nine-

35 teenth-and twentieth-century French paintings, whose creators were influenced by Japanese art? And what of the cubists, through whom the influence of African art changed modern painting, or the surrealists, who were so impressed with the art of the Pacific Northwest Indians that, in their map of North America, Alaska dwarfs the lower forty-eight in size?

40   When I heard a schoolteacher warn the other night about the invasion of the American educational system by foreign curriculums, I wanted to yell at the television set, "Lady, they're already here." It has already begun because the world is here. The world has been arriving at these shores for at least ten thousand years from Europe, Africa, and Asia. In the late nine-

45 teenth and early twentieth centuries, large numbers of Europeans arrived, adding their cultures to those of the European, African, and Asian settlers who were already here, and recently millions have been entering the country from South America and the Caribbean, making Yale professor Bob Thompson's bouillabaisse richer and thicker.

50   One of our most visionary politicians said that he envisioned a time when the United States would become the brain of the world, by which he meant the repository of all of the latest advanced information systems. I thought of that remark when an enterprising poet friend of mine called to say that he had just sold a poem to a computer magazine and that the editors

55 were delighted to get it because they didn't carry fiction or poetry. Is that the kind of world we desire? A humdrum homogeneous world of all brains and no heart, no fiction no poetry; a world of robots with human attendants

Source: Excerpted from *Writin' is Fightin'*

bereft of imagination, of culture? Or does North America deserve a more exciting destiny? To become a place where the cultures of the world criss-
60 cross. This is possible because the United States is unique in the world: The world is here.

Check Your Comprehension

1. What is the purpose of the quotation from the *New York Times* that precedes this reading?

2. Why does Reed feel the idea of "Western civilization" is misleading?

3. What is meant by "cultural bouillabaisse"? Why does Reed like this idea?

READING

Find out more about **understanding long sentences** by looking in the Reference Guide to Reading Strategies on pages xii–xiv.

Understanding Long Sentences

Reed uses long sentences in several places in this writing. For example:

The result is what the Yale professor, Robert Thompson, referred to as a cultural bouillabaisse, yet members of the nation's present educational and cultural elect still cling to the notion that the United States belongs to some vaguely defined entity they refer to as "Western civilization," by which they mean, presumably, a civilization created by the people of Europe, as if Europe can be viewed in monolithic terms.

These can be difficult to follow when reading. It might help to think of these sentences in terms of phrases, or separate sentences. For example, the sentence above might be rewritten as follows:

The result is what the Yale professor, Robert Thompson, referred to as a cultural bouillabaisse. However, members of the nation's present educational and cultural elect still cling to the notion that the United States belongs to some vaguely defined entity they refer to as "Western civilization." This means, presumably, a civilization created by the people of Europe, as if Europe can be viewed in monolithic terms.

Identify three other long sentences in the passage that might be difficult to understand. On the lines provided, rewrite each of them as a series of shorter sentences. Be sure that each sentence is complete and correct—no fragments! Look up any words you don't understand.

1. Original: _____

_____

_____

_____

_____

_____

Rewrite: _____

_____

_____

_____

_____

2. Original: _____

_____

_____

_____

_____

Rewrite: _____

_____

_____

_____

3. Original: _____

_____

_____

_____

_____

Rewrite: _____

_____

_____

_____

_____

VOCABULARY
Using New Words

Complete the following sentences, showing that you understand the meaning of the word in italics.

1. Our course *curriculum* includes _____

2. "American culture" is not *monolithic* because _____

3. I had a rather *humdrum* afternoon. I _____

4. A *surrealist* artist _____

5. My brother is very *enterprising;* for example he _____

THINK ABOUT IT

1. Many *metaphors* have been used to refer to America's multiculturalism. Think about each of the following metaphors. Then, write about or discuss what each means, and the image it presents.

   > *melting pot*
   >
   > *tossed salad*
   >
   > *mosaic*
   >
   > *cultural bouillabaisse*

   Now, think of an additional metaphor that captures what U.S. multiculturalism means to you.

2. Write a short description of any multicultural influences there have been on your culture. Think not only of the current society, but of its history as well. Describe what you know to your class.

PART TWO

Housing: A Roof Over One's Head

This part of the chapter talks about the importance of housing to many Americans. Even though Americans frequently move to new homes, they still have strong feelings about their homes, as you will see in the next two readings.

Before You Read

"Owning one's home has long been considered a part of the American Dream. If so, we have been much better off in recent decades than we were in the early twentieth century. In 1990, about 64 percent of American households owned their own homes; at the dawn of the century, less than half could make that claim."

Home Ownership 1900–1990

1900	1910	1920	1930	1940	1950	1960	1970	1980	1990
46.5%	45.9%	45.6%	47.8%	43.6%	55.0%	61.9%	62.9%	64.4%	64.2%

Source: (of quotation and statistics): U.S. Bureau of the Census, Census of Housing

This reading addresses the issue of home ownership in the United States. It comes from a speech given by President Bill Clinton in 1996. In it he explains the importance of home ownership to many Americans.

Before you read, think about the following questions:

- Do you think home ownership is important? Why or why not?
- Do you know what percentage of people in your country own their own homes?

Cultural Cues

private sector The part of the workforce that does not work for the government

About the Author   Bill Clinton is the forty-second President of the United States.

National Home Ownership

by President Bill Clinton

June 6, 1996

I want to thank all of you in the private sector who worked for a year with our national home ownership strategy and those of you who worked for a lifetime to help people realize the dream of owning their own home.

5　　When I became President I saw this mission of expanding home ownership as part of our larger goal of restoring economic opportunity and a sense of security to Americans who are working hard and trying to build families and raise children. The fact that home ownership had stagnated for several years, to me, was just another indication of why we needed to

10　get our economy moving and working for ordinary people again.

I think everybody here, of whatever age, remembers the first home you bought. Some of you heard me tell this story before, but I had to buy a home to get married. Hillary and I had been going together for several years and we were living in Fayetteville, Arkansas, and we were both teaching at

15　the University law school. And she was going away on some trip—she was always getting trips to go away on. And she—I took her to the airport one day. We passed this old house.

She said, boy, that's a pretty house. I said, it really is. So I took her to the airport, went back and checked on the house. It was 1,100 square feet,

20　it cost $20,500. And it was a beautiful little house—no air-conditioning, attic fan, hardwood floors. And I bought the house. And I made whatever the down payment was. I remember my mortgage payment was $174 a month.

And so, three or four days later, she came back from her trip and I said, you know that house you like so well? I said, I bought that house. Now,

25　don't you think you'll have to marry me so I won't have to live there by myself? I am a living example of the power of home ownership to strengthen families and build better futures.

Home ownership is now at a 15-year high, and last year the increase was the highest rate of increase in home ownership in almost 30 years. And

30　one of the things that I also want to point out that I'm very proud of is that home ownership is more broadly distributed now in America than it has been in a long time. There's been a very rapid increase in the number of African American first-time home owners, very rapid increase in the number of Hispanic home owners, an increase in the number of working women

35　with children who own their own homes now.

So we are working hard to broaden the benefits of that. And so many of you are a big part of that. Sixty-five percent of the American people now own their own homes. Our goal is to go from 3.7 million new home owners to 8 million new home owners by the year 2000, bringing us to over 67

40　percent of the American people or two-thirds of the American people that own homes by the year 2000—the first time that has ever been achieved in the history of this country. Together, you and I—all of us working together—we can achieve that goal. And I think we ought to recommit ourselves to it today.

Check Your Comprehension

1. In the speech, the President says, "those of you who worked for a lifetime." To whom is he speaking, in your opinion?

2. Why does President Clinton want to increase home ownership?

3. Why did President Clinton buy his first house?

4. What does the President mean when he says that home ownership is more "broadly distributed" now?

 **READING**

Find out more about **summarizing** by looking in the Reference Guide to Reading Strategies on pages xii–xiv.

Summarizing

Summarizing what you read can help you to understand an essay more fully. In this speech, each paragraph has a main idea. In the following space, write a summary of the speech by writing a summary sentence for each paragraph. Refer to the article to help you understand his main points. The first one is done for you.

Paragraph 1. The President thanks his audience for helping others to reach their dream of owning a home.

Paragraph 2. _____

_____

Paragraph 3. _____

_____

Paragraph 4. _____

_____

Paragraph 5. _____

_____

Paragraph 6. _____

_____

Paragraph 7. _____

_____

Compare your summary sentences with those written by a classmate. What information did you include that he or she did not?

VOCABULARY
Using New Vocabulary

Complete the following sentences, showing that you understand the **bold-faced** word.

1. In my opinion, an important government **mission** is _____

    _____

2. If the economy **stagnates,** it _____

    _____

3. If you have a **mortgage** you must _____

    _____

4. A **down payment** is _____

    _____

5. We should **recommit** ourselves to _____

    _____

THINK ABOUT IT

1. Many Americans place a high value on owning a home. Do you agree with this value? Why or why not?

2. What are the attitudes toward home ownership in your home country?

3. Think about the advantages and disadvantages of owning your own home. If you don't own a home, would you like to? Why or why not? Fill in the table below, and then, based on what you wrote, explain to your partner why you would or wouldn't want to own a home.

Advantages of Owning a Home	Disadvantages of Owning a Home

Before You Read   Recent Movers

"In the second half of this century, we Americans have been prone to change homes frequently, especially those of us who rent. For the last four censuses, about 40 percent of renter households were recent movers. But, owners move also; about 1 in 10 were recent movers."

Year	Total of Recent Movers: Owners	Percent of Recent Movers: Owners	Total of Recent Movers: Renters	Percent of Recent Movers: Renters
1960	4,011,702	12.2%	7,774,224	38.4%
1970	4,288,403	10.8%	9,372,311	39.8%
1980	6,126,736	11.8%	12,135,188	42.4%
1990	5,524,646	9.4%	13,683,377	41.6%

Source: U.S. Bureau of the Census, Census of Housing, Recent Movers

In this reading, the author discusses a common event in many Americans' lives—selling their homes and moving.

Before you read, think about the following questions:

- Have you or your family ever moved to a new home? What was the experience like?

- What is the difference, in your opinion, between a house and a home?

About the Author

Andy Rooney began his writing career as a correspondent for *The Stars and Stripes*, a military newspaper, during World War II. Since then, he has written for television and many newspapers. He is currently well known for his short, humorous weekly contribution to the television news program *60 Minutes*.

Home

by Andy Rooney

One Saturday night we were sitting around our somewhat shopworn living room with some old friends when one of them started trying to remember how long we'd lived there.

"Since 1952," I said. "We paid off the mortgage eight years ago."

5 "If you don't have a mortgage," he said, "the house isn't worth as much as if you did have one."

Being in no way clever with money except when it comes to spending it, this irritated me.

"To whom is it not worth as much," I asked him in a voice that was 10 louder than necessary for him to hear what I was saying. "Not to me, and I'm the one who lives here. As a matter of fact, I like it about fifty percent more than I did when the bank owned part of it."

"What did you pay for it?" he asked.

"We paid $29,500 in 1952."

15 My friend nodded knowingly and thought a minute.

"I'll bet you," he said, "that you could get $85,000 for it today . . . you ought to ask $95,000."

I don't know why this is such a popular topic of conversation these days, but if any real estate dealers are reading this, I'll give them some money-20 saving advice. Don't waste any stamps on me with your offers to buy. You can take me off your mailing list.

Our house is not an investment. It is not a hastily erected shelter in which to spend the night before we rise in the morning to forge on farther west to locate in another campsite at dusk. Our house is our home. We live 25 there. It is an anchor. It is the place we go to when we don't feel like going anyplace.

We do not plan to move.

The last census indicated that forty million Americans move every year. One out of every five packs up his things and goes to live somewhere else.

30 Where is everyone moving to? Why are they moving there? Is it really better someplace else?

If people want a better house, why don't they fix the one they have?

If the boss says they're being transferred and have to move, why don't they get another job? Jobs are easier to come by than a home. I can't imagine 35 giving up my home because my job was moving.

I have put up twenty-nine Christmas trees in the bay window of the living room, each a little too tall. There are scars on the ceiling to prove it.

Behind the curtain of the window nearest my wife's desk, there is a vertical strip of wall four inches wide that has missed the last four coats
40 of paint so that the little pencil marks with dates opposite them would not be obliterated. If we moved, someone would certainly paint that patch and how would we ever know again how tall the twins were when they were four?

My son Brian has finished college and is working and no longer lives at
45 home, but his marbles are in the bottom drawer of his dresser if he ever wants them.

There's always been talk of moving. As many as ten times a year we talk about it. The talk was usually brought on by a leaky faucet, some peeling paint, or a neighbor we didn't like.

50 When you own a house you learn to live with its imperfections. You accommodate yourself to them and, like your own shortcomings, you find ways to ignore them.

Our house provides me with a simple pleasure every time I come home to it. I am welcomed by familiar things when I enter, and I'm warmed by
55 some ambience which may merely be dust, but it is our dust and I like it. There are reverberations of the past everywhere, but it is not a sad place, because all the things left undone hold great hope for its future.

The talk of moving came up at dinner one night ten years ago. Brian was only half listening, but at one point he looked up from his plate, gazed
60 around the room and asked idly, "Why would we want to move away from home?"

When anyone asks me how much I think our house is worth, I just smile. They couldn't buy what that house means to me for all the money in both local banks.

Source: Excerpt from *And More by Andy Rooney* 65 The house is not for sale.

Check Your Comprehension

1. What is the author's definition of *home?*

2. Why does he say that he does not want to move?

3. What is the meaning of the "little pencil marks with dates"?

 **READING**

Find out more about **finding and understanding the main idea** by looking in the Reference Guide to Reading Strategies on pages xii–xiv.

Finding and Understanding the Main Idea

What is the main idea of this article? State it in one sentence.

_____

_____

_____

_____

List three reasons that Rooney uses to support this main idea.

1. _____

_____

_____

2. _____

_____

_____

3. _____

_____

_____

VOCABULARY
Two-Word Verbs

Choose the correct phrase for each of the sentences below. You may have to change the form of the verb (for example, add -s, -ed, etc.). Note that the verb and the preposition may be separated in some sentences.

pay off	*pay for*	*take off*	*put up*	*bring on*
give up	*come up*	*move away*	*pack up*	*come by*

1. I need to _____ my debts _____ before I buy a new house.

2. If you move out of your house, you should _____ your

name _____ the mailbox.

3. Before leaving, he _____ his belongings.

4. Beatrice _____ her new furniture with a credit card.

5. We couldn't afford to move, so we _____ with some new ideas for fixing our old house.

6. In general, you should not _____ your old apartment before you find a new one.

7. My father always _____ the holiday decorations _____ every December.

8. My daughter was sad when we had to _____ from our old house.

9. You don't _____ a good house every day—you should buy that one immediately!

10. I don't know what _____ his anger _____. Maybe he's tired of his noisy neighbors.

THINK ABOUT IT

1. The author says that new jobs are easier to find than new homes. Do you agree? Why or why not?

2. When a population moves frequently, does it have an effect on the society? Explain your opinion.

3. Does your first language have different words for *house* and *home*? In your journal, write about these words and what they mean in your first language. Then, write a paragraph explaining the difference between these two words in English.

4. Look at these classified advertisements, which feature homes for sale. Try to determine what the abbreviations in the ads mean by choosing the correct house(s) for each of the ten questions. The first one is done for you.

a. Amesbury, Prestigious Highlands area lovely 3 BR Col., new fully applc. kit., new electric, hdwd. flrs., deck, nat'l woodwork, full bsmt., built-in hutch in DR. $175K.	**b. Concord,** Lovely 10 rm., 5 BR, 2 1/2 bath Col. on cul-de-sac w/2.8 acres, slate foyer opens up to lg. LR w/frpl., library/study. DR & lg. FR. $495K.	**c. Haverhill,** Quality condo, priv. fenced yard, pressure treated deck, lg. kit., abundant cbnt. space, 1 1/2 baths, 2 BRs, bsmt. $89.5K.

d. Reading, Surrounded by flowering shrubs & trees this lovely mint cond. home has 4 BRs, 2 baths, formal DR, sunrm. & very priv. pool area. $319.9K	**e. Wakefield,** Well maintained Col. in great loc. Dynamite kit., frpl., LR, hdwd. flrs., 2 car gar., central air & ingrd. pool. $189.9K

	a.	b.	c.	d.	e.
1. Which house(s) are in the Colonial style of architecture?	X	X	__	__	X
2. Which house is the cheapest?	__	__	__	__	__
3. Which house is the most expensive?	__	__	__	__	__
4. Which house(s) have wood floors?	__	__	__	__	__
5. Which house(s) have a fireplace?	__	__	__	__	__
6. Which house(s) have a pool?	__	__	__	__	__
7. Which house(s) have a dining room?	__	__	__	__	__
8. Which house(s) have a garage?	__	__	__	__	__
9. Which house(s) have a lot of cabinet space?	__	__	__	__	__
10. Which house has the most bedrooms?	__	__	__	__	__
11. Which house(s) have a sunroom?	__	__	__	__	__

S Y N T H E S I S

Discussion and Debate

1. Many people argue that the United States is too crowded and that immigration should be stopped or cut back drastically. What is your opinion? Explain your reasons clearly.

2. How do U.S. homes and homes in your home country compare? If you don't know about a U.S. home, interview someone who lives in a "typical" American home. Fill out the table below, then discuss your answers with your classmates.

   Here are some features to consider: size, number, arrangement of furniture, and so forth.

Areas	United States	My home country
kitchen		
living room		

Areas	United States	My home country
bedroom		
garage		
garden		
bathroom		
Other:		
Other:		
Other:		
Other:		

3. What would your ideal home be like?

4. Think of an additional question to ask your classmates about something in this chapter. (Ask for ideas and opinions rather than specific information from the reading.)

Writing Topics

1. Does this chapter present any ideas or opinions with which you strongly agree or disagree? Write a paragraph in your journal about your opinions.

2. Write a letter to a friend in your home city describing the home and possessions of an American you have met. (If you have not met any Americans, you can invent one to write about.)

3. Before visiting a new place, most people have certain beliefs about it, perhaps from reading or from speaking to others. However, after they arrive, they might find the place different from what they expected. Write a short essay explaining what you thought the United States would be like before you arrived. Then, describe the things that were the same and the things that were different from what you expected.

On Your Own

1. Look at recent newspapers in the library or on the Internet. Look for articles or editorials about United States immigration. Read one or two articles and summarize them. Then, write a paragraph of your own opinion about the article.

2. Conduct a survey of Americans on the topics of immigration and housing. Speak to at least ten people. Summarize your results in writing. Here are some questions you may start with. Add your own questions if you wish.

   • How many times have you moved from one house to another in your lifetime?

   • Do you own or rent your house?

   • Did your family immigrate to the United States? If so, when?

   • From what country (countries) does your family come?

   Compare your results with the results from your classmates. Are there differences? If so, why do you think those differences exist?

3. The films *Green Card, Moscow on the Hudson,* and *El Norte* all deal with the subject of immigration to the United States. Choose one of these films and check it out from the library or a video store. Write a short essay about the film. How did it compare to the readings in this chapter?

★★★

A L M A N A C For additional cultural information, refer to the Almanac on pages 221–234. The Almanac contains lists of useful facts, maps, and other information to enhance your learning.

★★★

CHAPTER 2

Money

The United States is a wealthy nation. Its success in business is known worldwide. How does its population contribute to its wealth? What effect does wealth have on the American people? This chapter looks at American success in the business world, and the impact of credit cards on Americans.

PART ONE

THE ECONOMY
Business: Show Me the Money!

What does it take to have a successful American business? Some businesses become so popular they are associated with America itself. McDonald's, now a globally successful chain, is one such business. This section looks at two other successful American businesses.

Before You Read

This table shows what different segments of the U.S. population earned in 1996.

Income 1996

Characteristics	Average Income
All households	$35,492
Race and Origin of Householder	
White	$37,161
Black	$23,482
Asian or Pacific Islander	$43,276
Hispanic origins	$24,906
Type of Household	
Married-couple households with related children under 18	$51,894
Female householder, no husband present with related children under 18	$18,261
Age of Household Members	
With members 65 years old and over	$20,985
With related children under 18	$41,955

Source: The U.S. Bureau of the Census, Income 1996

In the following reading, Howard Schultz, the head of Starbucks coffee, answers questions about his very popular business. Before you read, think about these questions:

- Have you heard of Starbucks coffee?
- Why do you think this is such a successful company?

Cultural Cues

CEO The head of a company, its **C**hief **E**xecutive **O**fficer.

decaf doppios Decaffeinated double espresso coffee.

deep pockets A large source of money.

megachain Extremely large ('mega') chain of stores.

munchies Snacks.

skinny latte Espresso with non-fat milk added.

sound bites Short commercials or pieces of video used to promote a product or political candidate.

warp speed Very fast speed.

Making Customers Come Back for More:
How Starbucks Created a Brand on a Budget

An Interview with Howard Schultz

Talk about a guy who rarely has time to take a coffee break. In the past ten years, Starbucks Corp. Chairman and CEO Howard Schultz
5 has grown a six-store Seattle coffee-bean retailer into a $1 billion megachain of Italian-style coffee bars. What's
10 in this tale for the small-business operator? For one thing, 43-year-old Schultz didn't have the deep pockets to build
15 his brand, and he figures other small companies can do it the same way he did. Over a cup of espresso in his office,
20 Schultz told our Lori Ioannou his secrets:

How do you transform a common cup of coffee into a gourmet product?

The goal was to add value to a commodity
25 typically purchased on supermarket aisles. Our so-called baristas [bartenders] introduce customers to the fine coffees of
30 the world the way wine stewards bring forward fine wines. They explain the different flavors and
35 characteristics of coffees like Sumatra, Sulawesi, and Ethiopia Sidamo. They also introduce
40 great-tasting specialty drinks— brews like decaf doppios and skinny lattes. Eventually patrons become coffee con-
45 noisseurs, and they keep coming back for another cup.

You've made Starbucks the IBM of coffee at warp speed and without many ads. How did you pull that off?

45 Since I bought the business in 1987, we've spent less than $10 million on advertising. Not because I didn't believe in it, but because I couldn't afford it. Instead we concentrated on creating value and customer service. Starbucks
50 store managers and workers have been the best ambassadors for the brand. They make personal attachments with customers, who have spread the word. For many of our customers, the Starbucks coffeehouse is an extension of
55 their front porch, a comforting place to hang out and enjoy a drink, munchies, and friends. Our success proves you can build a national brand without 30-second sound bites.

Tell us how you're leveraging your brand
60 *beyond the stores.*

You'll find Starbucks coffee at airports, bookstores, and hotels, and 30,000 feet above ground. Our goal is to make our coffee available where people shop, travel, play, and work
65 so it bursts into the national consciousness. We've formed alliances with a long list of companies, from Barnes & Noble to Costco stores to ITT/ Sheraton and Westin hotels, Horizon and United Airlines. Each now distributes our
70 coffee in a different way. United Airlines serves it on all of its flights. Barnes & Noble has carved out areas within its bookstores to set up Star-

bucks coffee shops; Westin offers lodgers complimentary Starbucks coffee packs that can be
75 brewed in their rooms.

What new products have you spun out to capitalize on the Starbucks name?

We're now selling Starbucks premium coffee ice cream and a bottled version of our Frap-
80 puccino beverage at supermarkets across America. This spring we will also start selling our coffee beans and ground coffee at grocery stores in ten major cities, including Denver and Los Angeles. The plan is to capture a
85 20% share of the $1 billion specialty-coffee retail market.

It seems there would be some danger from overexposure. How are you going to avoid it?

90 I don't think we are cannibalizing ourselves as long as we continue to introduce and offer best-of-class products. So far we've been successful. In fact, three months after we introduced our Starbucks gourmet ice cream
95 nationally with flavors like JavaChip, we became the No. 1 premium coffee ice cream in the country. I believe the way to stay on top is to continually reinvent yourself, and that is exactly what Starbucks does with its
100 brand and products.

Source: *Fortune Magazine* on-line

Check Your Comprehension

1. How did Starbucks change the way Americans view coffee?

2. Does Starbucks advertise much? How do consumers get to know their products?

3. How is Schultz making Starbucks popular outside of the Starbucks coffee shops?

4. Why isn't he afraid of overexposure?

READING

Find out more about **summarizing** by looking in the Reference Guide to Reading Strategies on pages xii–xiv.

Summarizing

In this interview, Schultz talks about many of the things that he believes led to Starbucks' great success. Summarize that information by answering the questions below.

What is the Starbucks approach to . . .

1. redefining the product? _____

_____

_____

2. advertising and publicity? _____

_____

_____

_____

3. selling coffee outside the store? _____

_____

_____

_____

4. creating new products? _____

_____

_____

VOCABULARY
Learning from Context

The following words are used in the reading. Look at the context of each word or phrase. Circle other words or phrases that give you a hint about the meaning. Then, write what you think the words mean. The first one is done for you. (If the sentences below don't give you enough context, review the entire reading again.)

1. For one thing, 43-year-old Schultz didn't have the <u>deep pockets</u> to build his brand, and he figures other small companies can do it the same way he did.

    Deep pockets means "a lot of money" in this context. The clue is the word "build" which says he needs something to make his company work. "A lot of money" makes sense, because that's what you need to expand a company.

2. You've made Starbucks the IBM of coffee at <u>warp speed</u> and without many ads. How did you <u>pull that off</u>?

_____

_____

_____

3. Since I bought the business in 1987, we've spent less than $10 million on advertising. . . . Starbucks store managers and workers . . . make personal attachments with customers, who have <u>spread the word</u>. . . . Our success proves you can build a national brand without 30-second <u>sound bites</u>.

_____

_____

_____

4. Tell us how you're <u>leveraging</u> your brand beyond the stores.

_____

_____

_____

5. Barnes & Noble has <u>carved out</u> areas within its bookstores to set up Starbucks coffee shops; Westin offers lodgers complimentary Starbucks coffee packs that can be brewed in their rooms.

_____

_____

_____

6. What new products have you <u>spun out</u> to <u>capitalize on</u> the Starbucks name?

_____

_____

_____

7. It seems there would be some danger from <u>overexposure.</u> How are you going to avoid it?

_____

_____

_____

8. I don't think we are <u>cannibalizing ourselves</u> as long as we continue to introduce and offer best-of-class products. . . . I believe the way to stay on top is to continually <u>reinvent yourself,</u> and that is exactly what Starbucks does with its brand and products.

_____

_____

_____

THINK ABOUT IT

1. One of the complaints about Starbucks is that it drives small, independent coffee houses out of business. Should small businesses be protected, in your opinion? Why or why not?

2. Why do you think chain restaurants like Starbucks and McDonald's are so popular?

3. Do you visit chain restaurants? Which ones? Why? (If you don't, why not?)

Before You Read

Some of Ben & Jerry's Ice Cream Flavors

Cherry Garcia® Ice Cream Sweet ice cream with bing cherries and dark chocolate chunks.

Chocolate Chip Cookie Dough Ice Cream Cookie dough flavored ice cream with gobs of raw (pasteurized) chocolate chip cookie dough.

Chubby Hubby Ice Cream® Chocolate-covered peanut butter-filled pretzels in vanilla malt ice cream rippled with fudge and peanut butter.

Chunky Monkey® Ice Cream Banana ice cream made from banana puree with walnuts and dark chocolate chunks.

Coffee, Coffee BuzzBuzzBuzz! ™ ***Ice Cream*** Espresso roast coffee ice cream with espresso bean-flecked dark chocolate chunks.

Coffee Olé ™ ***Ice Cream*** Rich coffee ice cream made with coffee from rural Mexico's Aztec Harvests farmers.

Cool Britannia ™ ***Ice Cream*** Vanilla ice cream with strawberries and chocolate-covered shortbread.

Holy Cannoli® Ice Cream A blend of vanilla, ricotta and pistachio ice cream with pistachios and cocoa-coated cannoli pieces.

Pistachio Pistachio Ice Cream Pistachio ice cream with lightly roasted, salted pistachios.

Phish Food ™ ***Ice Cream*** Chocolate ice cream with a marshmallow nougat and caramel swirl and fudge fish.

Rainforest Crunch® Ice Cream Vanilla ice cream with chunks of Rainforest Crunch®, a cashew and Brazil nut butter crunch.

Wavy Gravy™ Ice Cream Caramel cashew Brazil nut ice cream with a chocolate hazelnut fudge swirl and roasted almonds.

Source: http://www.benjerry.com

In the following reading, the author describes the successful U.S. company, Ben & Jerry's ice cream.

Before you read, think about the following questions:

- Have you ever eaten any of these flavors of ice cream? What was it like?

- What do you think the title, "Caring Capitalism," means?

Cultural Cues

In the beginning . . . This is a reference to the beginning of the Old Testament of the Judeo-Christian bible.

401(k) plan A retirement savings plan

Ben & Jerry's: Caring Capitalism

by Jennifer J. Laabs

In the beginning was the cow. The cow grazed along the grassy hillsides of Vermont and made milk. And it was good.

Then two best buddies, Ben and Jerry, came
5 along and used the milk to make superpremium ice cream and frozen yogurt. And it was great. So they made money—lots of it.

And as the cosmos aligned in perfect harmony, Ben and Jerry created a company to
10 make the ice cream and said. "Let it be a workers' paradise and let it be fun."

And from this ideal, a human resources [HR] department emerged to give form and shape to the company's culture. And HR
15 breathed life into a corporate environment that places a great value on each employee, rewards workers substantially for their labor and encourages them to give something of themselves back to their community. It also cheers employ-
20 ees on to have fun while they pursue the almighty paycheck.

And that was positively otherworldly.

It would be tempting to rest after spending so much energy creating such a brave new
25 world. But Ben & Jerry's is a company with a unique mission: to do more than just make ice cream. It also strives to make a difference in the world. The company measures its success by how much it gives back to the community—
30 locally, nationally and internationally. The organization even refers to the dual bottom line in its mission statement: to be profitable for its shareholders and to be socially responsible, inside and outside the organization.

35 And that, actually, was outstanding—especially for Ben & Jerry's employees. The company not only provides compensation and benefits that rank with America's largest em-

ployers, but it also takes the employment relationship a step beyond just handing out pay-
checks. It holds "a deep respect for individuals
. . . and for the communities of which they are
a part."

For Vermont, the organization is big. It has
400 workers, placing it among the state's top
10 employers. In revenue, it's also big—$100
million in 1991, and growing.

Although some employees at Ben & Jerry's
must take on a greater responsibility than
others, what distinguishes the work environment is the fact that employees are treated and
rewarded fairly. Every employee's opinion is
sought out and valued.

Fun is a corporate mantra. Jerry Green-
field, the company's 41-year-old cofounder and
self-proclaimed minister of joy, often has been
quoted as saying: "If it's not fun, why do it?" So,
amid the fury of ice-cream making (they can't
make it fast enough to supply the demand in the
38 states in which it's distributed), everyone
can expect to have some fun while they work.

That's why, in 1988, Green-
field created the Joy Gang, a rov-
ing band of merrymakers, who,
at any given moment, may be
seen celebrating those lesser-
known holidays, like national
clashdressing Day. This holiday provides the unfashion-
conscious workers with a
chance to show off their stuff—
exaggerated to the limit, of
course. On clash day, the most
outrageous outfits are rewarded
with such prizes as glow-in-the-
dark religious statues and rub-
ber crustaceans.

Linked prosperity is the basis
of compensation. The organization's compensation philosophy
always has been one of linked
prosperity—if the company does
well, they all do well. Ben & Jerry's, which was founded in 1978,
has even outlined this philosophy in the company's mission statement. The organization
maintains what it calls a "fair ratio" between
the lowest and highest salaries. In 1990, the
ratio was changed from 5:1 to 7:1, basically
resulting from growing pains: The company
had grown and the salary structure no longer
fit. (The ratio calculation is determined by adding the lowest wage for a full-time employee—
employed for at least one year—to the value
of the benefits.)

The work environment is employee-oriented. In the summer, many employees wear
shorts, and T-shirts are a wardrobe must. In
the winter, they wear jeans. You'd be hard-
pressed to find anyone at the company who
owns a tie, including the cofounders.

Just because they don't wear suits and don't
have a dress code doesn't mean they aren't
serious about what they do. They just happen
to be extremely comfortable while they're
doing it.

Communication also is important at Ben &

Jerry's—and it goes both ways. Every six weeks to two months, staff meetings are held. The company founders often attend, and can be seen telling jokes and giving pertinent information about what's happening inside the world of Ben & Jerry's.

"We actually can talk to Ben and Jerry, and they tell us what's going on. We do a lot of listening at these meetings. They're very informative and help us know what's happening," says Julie Labor, one of the company's production line workers in the Waterbury plant.

At other organizations, she says, she didn't even know the company leaders' names. "They probably were just sitting at home collecting a paycheck. I don't know. I never saw them," says Labor.

Ben & Jerry's also has designated half of the proceeds it collects from tours of its manufacturing facility in Waterbury for what's called the Entrepreneurial Fund. This fund awards low-interest loans to people starting new businesses, including employees. To receive funding, the new business must have a socially correct theme.

The other half of the money from tours goes to the Employee Community Fund Committee (comprising rank-and-file employees), which meets monthly to evaluate requests for money, and to award cash grants to local causes.

On the home front, any Ben & Jerry's employee may volunteer to work in his or her community and be paid the normal rate for this work. "Interested employees are invited to design their own community volunteer program. It's limited to a total of five employees performing 50 hours of community service each year," says Chaplin.

To help the global community, whenever possible, the company tries to buy ingredients for its ice cream that support a philosophy of "caring capitalism." For example, cashew and Brazil nuts are purchased from native forest people in Brazil, who now earn three to 10 times their previous income—a more lucrative venture than deforestation. Also, the blueberries the company purchases are grown by Maine's Passamaquoddy Indians, and this helps support economic development among Native Americans.

In the production area, employees listen to music, which rotates between one of the three stations that are broadcast in the area. "Actually, the Joy Gang bought our stereo. We listen to music and enjoy our work." says Labor.

"In most factories like this, you can't play music at all," says Scott Sandifer, production manager at the company's Waterbury plant and Labor's supervisor. He's worked at several other manufacturing plants and says he has never seen any other plants that allowed music in the production area. "Here we have speakers mounted on the ceiling. It's cooking at a good volume. It's nice," he says.

Although this helps improve working conditions, Sandifer points out that it's still production-line work. "It's a hard job. We try to make the environment as relaxed as we can, but the work is still hard," he says.

While their parents work, some employees' children spend the day at the company's children's center—another benefit that enables workers to balance work and family life. The center is in a renovated farmhouse on land adjacent to the company's headquarters. A gentle stream runs quietly behind the property.

During the past six years, sales of Ben & Jerry's has increased tenfold. This has caused tremendous growth in the work force, and it's now moving from an entrepreneurial start-up to a professionally managed firm.

One issue with which Ben & Jerry's continually struggles is minority hiring and retention. Because Vermont's population is 98.6% Caucasian, it's difficult to find minority individuals locally. At the end of 1991, the company had only three African-American employees.

The company is diverse in other ways, however; 40% of the company's work force is female and three of the six senior managers are women. And the number of women in management is rising: Women also now hold five of

200 the 12 positions on the company's new quality council.

Does Ben & Jerry's bring out the best in employees? Do they appreciate the company? "When you've been treated so well, it's hard 205 not to appreciate it," says Labor. "And I'm not the only one—that's the best part about it. They do it for everyone. They really do go out of their way."

At Ben & Jerry's, quality is measured one 210 employee at a time. And it shows.

Source: Excerpted from *Personnel Journal*

Check Your Comprehension

1. What is meant by a "philosophy of caring capitalism"?

2. Name three benefits of working at Ben & Jerry's, according to the article.

3. Does Ben & Jerry's have any weaknesses as a company?

4. What is the plan for employee compensation (payment)?

5. In what ways is the work environment employee-oriented?

 **READING**

Find out more about **identifying topic sentences** by looking in the Reference Guide to Reading Strategies on pages xii–xiv.

Identifying Topic Sentences

This article is written in a *journalistic* style—a lot of short paragraphs. Most paragraphs have a topic sentence followed by support or examples of the topic. List six topic sentences from the reading here, then summarize the evidence the writer supplies for the topic. The first one is done for you.

Topic Sentence	Evidence
1. What distinguishes the work environment is the fact that employees are treated and rewarded fairly.	Every employee's opinion is sought out and valued.
2.	
3.	
4.	
5.	
6.	

VOCABULARY
Matching

Match each word on the left to its definition. Write the letter of the correct definition in the blank.

_____ **1.** *cosmos*   **a.** next to

_____ **2.** *entrepreneurial*   **b.** rebuilt

_____ **3.** *retention*   **c.** enterprise

_____ **4.** *adjacent*   **d.** relevant

_____ **5.** *pertinent*   **e.** clothing

_____ **6.** *renovated*   **f.** crab

_____ **7.** *venture*   **g.** solar system

_____ **8.** *lucrative*   **h.** holding

_____ **9.** *crustacean*   **i.** profitable

_____ **10.** *wardrobe*   **j.** capitalistic

THINK ABOUT IT

1. Would you like to work at Ben & Jerry's? What features make it an attractive workplace?

2. Why do you think more companies are *not* run like Ben & Jerry's?

3. How could Ben & Jerry's increase the number of minority employees?

4. Perform a taste test. Try one or two kinds of ice cream. Write a short description of the taste, and review how well you liked it. Combine your results with those of your classmates to produce a guide to different flavors of ice cream.

PART TWO

CREDIT: WHERE CREDIT IS DUE

The American public lives on credit cards. Many people have dozens of credit cards, and charge every purchase, from automobiles to loaves of bread. As a result, many Americans owe a lot of money to banks, and save less money than many people around the world.

Before You Read

Consumer Credit

This table shows the rate of savings and spending by American consumers in 1996 and 1997.

Income, Savings & Debt	Jun-96	Sep-96	Dec-96	Mar-97
Disposable Personal Income ($ billions of dollars)	5,595	5,656	5,735	5,851
Personal Savings Rate	5.3%	5.6%	5.3%	5.3%
Total Consumer Installment Credit	1,155.1	1,177.6	1,193.2	1,212.2

Source: The Federal Reserve Board, *Weekly Report*

In this reading, the author talks about the American habit of using credit cards, and some of the problems that go along with it.

Before you read, think about these questions:

- Do you have a credit card? Why or why not?
- What items have you bought on credit?

Cultural Cues

Frank Capra An American film director known for his sentimental movies about American life.

"It's a Wonderful Life," A Frank Capra film associated with Christmas.

Imelda Marcos Wife of former Philippine President Ferdinand Marcos; Imelda was known for her shopping habits.

Puritans and Quakers American religious groups, known for being frugal.

Thomas Jefferson One of the writers of the Declaration of Independence and the third President of the United States.

37

READING

Find out more about **active reading** by looking in the Reference Guide to Reading Strategies on pages xii–xiv.

Active Reading

This article from the *New York Times* has some difficult passages in it. It also has many facts that might amaze you. A good way to read an article like this is to read *actively*. That is, you should have a conversation in your head and on the page with the author.

As you read, make marks in the margins and on the text.

- Underline any word you don't understand, and put a ✓ in the margin.

- Put an **!** in the margin by any idea that you find interesting or amazing. Make a note about why you think it's interesting.

- Put an **X** in the margin by any idea that you disagree with. Write a note about your disagreement.

- Put a **?** in the margin by any idea you would like to discuss in class. Write your question in the margin, too.

Be prepared to talk about your markings in class.

GIVING CREDIT WHERE DEBT IS DUE

by Timothy L. O'Brien

As Frank Capra's mid-century holiday movie classic, "It's a Wonderful Life," crowds its way onto television screens, feel free to snicker at the moment when a des-
5 perate George Bailey screams at his negligent uncle for misplacing bank funds and threatening to plunge the family into debt.

"Where's that money?" he shouts. "Do you realize what this means? It means
10 bankruptcy and scandal and prison!"

Scandal? Prison? How quaint. America, safe haven of the highly leveraged country and the highly leveraged corporation, is now home to the highly leveraged citizen.
15 Debt is very, very cool.

Right now, consumers are firmly into debt overdrive as they pursue the annual rite of the holiday spending binge. Americans have even bestowed an affectionate
20 new term on their credit cards: "mall money."

That mall money is liberating, too. A recent survey of 1,000 consumers by the American Bankers Association found that
25 two-thirds had no holiday spending plan, even though they typically end up taking about six months to pay off holiday debt. And these are not poor people. The same survey found that among those who were
30 late with credit card payments, 44 percent earned more than $50,000 a year, while only 4 percent earned less than $15,000.

American consumers are carrying about $1.2 trillion in installment credit, up
35 about 50 percent from just four years ago, and the average credit card holder has four cards and about $4,000 in high-interest debt. Nonetheless, lenders have begun to

target the least creditworthy and most un-
sophisticated debtors-to-be, dubbing them
"sub-prime" borrowers. Loan delinquen-
cies are on the rise and personal bankrupt-
cies continue to soar.

But hey, why worry? Even bankruptcy
doesn't stop the solicitations from lenders.

Banks, which once upon a time empha-
sized savings and thrift, are now relentless
marketers of debt—or credit, to use the
sanitized term favored by lenders. Billions
of credit card solicitations compete for
space in American mailboxes each year,
with Banc One, MBNA, Citicorp, and Chase
Manhattan jointly account ing for more
than half of the volume.

Mortgages can be had for 125 percent
of a house's market value, quite a repudia-
tion of banks' traditional hesitation to lend
no more than 80 percent against a home.
Since late October, Fleet Financial Group
has mailed more than 1 million blank
checks in denominations ranging from
$3,000 to $10,000, inviting borrowers to use
the checks to pay taxes or "spruce up your
home."

"What debt is doing is that it anesthe-
tizes the purchasing process," said Stephen
M. Pollan, a financial adviser and author of
a new book, *Die Broke* (Harper Business).
"Debt may be OK for a house or a car or
an education, but for anything else you're
an idiot. For a bottle of champagne or a
new wardrobe you're going to go into debt?
It's just instant gratification, a short-lived
burst of fun, and it's not smart."

Debt is not the stigma it was for the
generation that came of age during the
Great Depression and World War II. So
when did things change?

Cultural milestones are never easy to
mark, but when it comes to consumer debt,
Fresno, Calif., in September 1958 offers a
likely one. Bank of America targeted
Fresno for the first mass mailing of credit
cards, as detailed by Joseph Nocera in *A*
Piece of the Action: How the Middle Class
Joined the Money Class (Simon & Schuster,
1994). Some 60,000 credit cards flooded the
mailboxes of Fresno. A little more than a
year later, 2 million credit cards were circu-
lating around California.

"There had been no outward yearning
among the residents of Fresno for such a
device, nor even the dimmest awareness
that such a thing was in the works," Nocera
wrote. "Here began the trickle of what we
now call financial products, aimed largely
at the middle class, that would become, by
the 1980s, an avalanche."

Still, in the 1960s most borrowers paid
off their credit card balances monthly, as
an aversion to financial risk born in the
Depression held sway. It would take another decade and the arrival of runaway
inflation to bring consumer debt into the
mainstream.

"Credit cards were the enablers but inflation was the trigger," Nocera said in an
interview. "People in the late 1970s started
recognizing that it made sense to go into
debt because of inflation."

America's trouble with debt is nothing
new. After all, Georgia was founded as a
debtors' colony, and Thomas Jefferson died
a debtor after a lifetime of buying binges
that would have made Imelda Marcos blush.

But for many years it was only an elite
few like Jefferson who could take on inordinate debt as consumers. Farmers and
other debtors largely borrowed in order to
produce something. Puritans and Quakers
regarded excessive personal debt as a sin,
views that were widely and firmly held until
relatively recently. In the 1800s, the end of
the year did not entail holiday shopping
sprees but was a time to pay off debts to
begin the new year with a clean slate and
a clean conscience.

"Debt was a horror in the 19th century,"
said Robert Sobel, a financial historian at
Hofstra University. "Mortgages were much

shorter in the 19th century, only about 10 years. Burning the mortgage was a big family event. Nowadays, people don't even think of mortgages as debt."

135 Of course, there weren't VCRs, Timberlands or Gap jeans to covet in the 19th and early 20th centuries. But once the emotional shock of the Depression subsided and the post-World War II consumer boom 140 occurred, Americans were primed to take a new look at debt. All they needed were credit cards and a nudge from those burgeoning inflation rates.

Now the costs are adding up. The con-145 sumer debt spigot has been wide open for the past five years and some borrowers are beginning to tread water, despite the robust economy. Several credit card companies, including such rapidly growing issuers as 150 Advanta, have taken a financial beating after coaxing risky borrowers with low in-

troductory teaser rates. Charge-offs for bad credit card debt have risen sharply this year at Advanta and other big credit card issu-155 ers. And if the economy slows significantly, America's penchant for debt may take an even uglier turn.

"People think about money in a certain way until a cataclysm arrives that forces 160 them to change," said Nocera, who added that it will probably take a sharp downturn in the economy before people think it wise to lighten their debt loads.

If this makes you queasy, just turn off 165 "It's a Wonderful Life" and tune in the Lifetime channel. There, every weeknight, you'll find a game show called "Debt," which gives contestants the opportunity to win enough money to rid themselves of 170 personal debt—uh, credit.

Source: The *New York Times*

Check Your Comprehension

1. How many credit cards does the average American have?
2. What is a "sub-prime" borrower?
3. What were the spending habits of people in the nineteenth and early twentieth centuries?
4. How has credit-card spending changed in the United States since the 1960s?

VOCABULARY
New Words

1. Look at the words you underlined in the reading, and list them here. (You don't have to fill all the blanks!)

_____   _____   _____   _____

_____   _____   _____   _____

_____   _____   _____   _____

_____   _____   _____   _____

_____   _____   _____   _____

2. Circle the words you could understand from context, and write a short definition for each of them on a separate piece of paper.
3. Compare the remaining words with a classmate's list. See if your lists of definitions can help with some of the words you still don't know.

4. Look up the rest of the words in a dictionary. Write the definitions on your paper.

5. Go back to the reading to be sure you understand all the words you underlined.

THINK ABOUT IT

 Watch the CNN video on consumer credit card use.

Discuss these questions:

1. What is the problem discussed in the video?

2. What are the warning signs that a consumer has this problem?

3. What suggestions does the video make?

1. What is your opinion of credit cards? Are they necessary? Do you know someone who has gotten into trouble because of credit card debt?

2. Do you receive credit card offers in the mail? What do you do with them?

3. Do some credit cards have more "status" than others? Which ones? Why do you think that is the case?

Before You Read

Discover Card advertisement

- **No Annual Fee**
- **Cashback Bonus® Award**
  Discover Card offers you something you can really use. . .CASH.
  Earn up to 1% based on your annual level of purchases, paid yearly.

And there's no limit each year, so the more you use your card, the higher your **Cashback Bonus Award.**

- **Tiered Interest Rates**
  Discover Card offers you an innovative way to help you spend more on yourself and less on interest. New Cardmembers receive our lowest variable interest rate (Prime Rate + 8.9%) on every purchase. And all Cardmembers can receive our award rate when they use their Discover Card for at least $1,000 in purchases a year and make timely payments.

- **Interest-Free Cash Advances**
  Never knowing when you'll need cash, it's nice to know you can get a Cash Advance with your Discover Card at ATM locations nationwide. And it's interest-free! Pay a small transaction fee and your balance in full each month, and you can get a Cash Advance Interest-Free for up to 25 days.

The author of this article looks humorously at the schemes that companies invent in order to get us to spend money.

Before you read, think about the following questions:

- Have you ever spent money on gifts or on a date to make someone like you?

- Do you belong to any "buyers' clubs" or "spend/save" plans?

Cultural Cues

Brobdingnagian Enormous, huge; this word comes from the classic book *Gulliver's Travels,* by Jonathan Swift. In that story there is a country called Brobdingnag, in which everything is enormous.

Postrio An expensive restaurant in San Francisco.

Merlot A type of red wine.

Sheryl Crow A popular American pop singer.

About the Author

Casey McCabe is a writer who lives in San Francisco.

I'm No Credit to Their Industry

by Casey McCabe

The letter opened pleasantly enough. *"Have you forgotten . . ."*

But I immediately detected a chill in the air.

". . . the many valuable advantages of your Brobdingnagian Bank Visa Card?"

5 And after all they've done for me. Fronting me the money when my car dropped its transmission on an abandoned logging road a few years back. Picking up that Postrio lunch tab after a few glasses of Merlot had me thinking I was Johnny Velvet. Those instant upgrades to their gold card, their platinum card and their new enriched plutonium card. And without

10 so much as a peep from me, they routinely include a $3,000 blank check in my statement along with the urgent encouragement: *Imagine, you could put it toward your child's college tuition, repanel your rec room, or why not run off to Aruba? Isn't it time* C. McCabe *started getting the most out of life?*

15 Maybe I have been something of a cad. I have no child, no rec room and no intention of running to Aruba, whoever she is, but that's hardly the bank's fault.

I'll never forget my first taste of plastic. It was a Visa, a debit card actually, meaning it went anywhere I wanted to go that my checking account

20 balance approved of. It established enough semblance of financial responsibility to secure me a real credit card later. Something about the blunt, unsolicitous nature of that card stayed with me. I remain almost freakishly resistant to spending money I don't have. At least one woman I dated took this as evidence that I would never love her enough. I suspect she is now

25 doing direct-mail marketing for banks.

A few years ago one such person must have come up with the brilliant idea that has since swept the industry. My new Visa card has given it an evangelical spin, calling the program Savings Redemption, but the concept is simple motivation: For every dollar you charge, you earn a rebate.

30 With the Visa from my phone company, every $100 I charge will earn me a $1 credit on my phone bill. My competing long-distance carrier has its own awards program, based on racking up extra hours on my phone bill to earn frequent-flier mileage on an airline that wants to issue me a Visa card of its own, which will reward me with more frequent-flier mileage and,

35 for all I know, rebates on my phone bill.

There was, however, enough basic logic in this new credit philosophy— *You're spending the money anyway,* C. McCabe, *why not get something back?*—to persuade me to sign up. Yet after a couple years I have been too paralyzed to reap the harvest of redemption I've so richly earned. What's

40 the proper reward for having charged several thousand dollars' worth of

goods and services? The free travel alarm clock? A Sheryl Crow CD? An upgrade from executive class to executive premier class?

Insidiously creeping into the mail are offerings from other entities, novice to both retail sales and consumer credit, but experts in guilt. Such as:

45   *Dear Alumni,*

We are pleased to offer you the services of the new Landgrant University Visa Card. It starts with a competitive interest rate and no annual fees. But it can do more. Much more. Because now each dollar you
50   *spend could be adding a brick to the proposed Social Engineering Center here at the university. A university, we might add, that gave you a degree when no one else could . . .*

My new credit suitors are by and large a noble bunch. They've all stum-
55   bled on the same benevolent concept that goes beyond shaving a few decimal points off the going interest rate, and they don't even call it a credit card anymore. They call it a savings card. The point they're really trying to drive home is: *The more you spend, the more you save!* Even the most forgiving semiotics experts would take this as a sign of mass societal delusion. But
60   chances are they already have their own travel alarm clocks.

Source: *San Francisco Chronicle*

Check Your Comprehension

1. What does the author mean by his "first taste of plastic"? Why does he remember it so fondly?

2. What is the "Savings Redemption" program the author describes?

3. Why does the author claim that the idea of "the more you spend, the more you save!" is a sign of "mass societal delusion"?

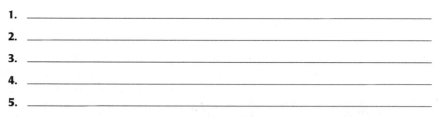

READING

Find out more about **understanding humor** by looking in the Reference Guide to Reading Strategies on pages xii–xiv.

Understanding Humor

The author uses sarcasm and exaggeration to make this a humorous reading. The first clue is the reference to "Brobdingnagian Bank Visa Card."

What other phrases or sentences use exaggeration or sarcasm? Try to find at least five, and write them here.

1. _____

2. _____

3. _____

4. _____

5. _____

Compare your list with a partner's list. Which examples are the same on both lists? Which are different? Do you agree with your partner's choices?

VOCABULARY
Slang and Colloquial Language

The following phrases are found in the reading. Can you determine what they mean? Fill in the blanks in the following sentences with the correct phrase. Note that sometimes you will have to separate some of the parts of the phrases. More than one may fit, but each one has a **best** answer.

front the money	*reap the harvest*
pick up the tab	*the going rate*
without a peep	*drive a point home*

1. He gave into my side _____ .

2. I need a loan. Can you _____ me _____?

3. If the bank lends me the money, it will be at _____ .

4. This meal is my treat. I'll _____ .

5. We saved our money for years, now we'll _____ .

6. When we argue, he really can _____ about his opinion.

THINK ABOUT IT

1. What are the advantages and disadvantages of using credit cards? Use the table below to list your thoughts. Then share your list with your classmates.

Advantages	Disadvantages
_____	_____
_____	_____
_____	_____

2. Find an advertisement for a buying club or a reward plan, such as for a credit card, frequent flyer program, or a telephone calling card. Bring the ad to class and explain to your classmates the benefits of the card. Also discuss how the ad presents information in a way to appeal to its audience.

3. Interview five people about their spending habits. Here are some questions you might want to use. You can add some of your own as well.

   • How many credit cards do you have?

   • Have you used your cards more this year than you did last year?

   • Do you normally buy things with cash or with a credit or debit card?

S Y N T H E S I S

Discussion and Debate

1. Some people might claim that Americans are too status-conscious; that is, money and possessions are too important to them. Do you agree? Why or why not? How does this situation compare with your own culture?

2. Although Americans have a reputation for being materialistic, there is also a strong tradition in the United States of charity, or donating money or possessions to people in need. In 1995, charitable contributions in the United States were $143.85 billion, according to statistics released in the annual "Giving USA" from the American Association of Fund-Raising Counsel (AAFRC) Trust for Philanthropy. Does this statistic surprise you? How can the qualities of materialism and charity co-exist? Does your own culture have a tradition of charity? Explain what it is.

3. There are two very different ways of handling money: one is to spend it when you get it; the other is to save as much as you can. How do you deal with money? Is one way better than the other? Why? What kind of attitude lies behind each philosophy?

4. Think of an additional question to ask your classmates about something in this chapter. (Ask for their ideas or opinions rather than specific information from the reading.)

Writing Topics

1. Does this chapter present any ideas or opinions with which you strongly agree or disagree? Write a paragraph about that idea.

2. Write a letter to a friend in which you explain what you have learned about American business in this chapter. Include your opinion on the ideas that you have thought about as well.

3. What is your opinion of credit card use? Write a short essay in which you defend your ideas.

On Your Own   1. One of the problems with credit cards is identity theft, that is, someone using your identification to get credit cards, and then spending large sums of money. On the Internet or in newspapers and magazines, see if you can find some information about this crime. Write instructions for how to protect yourself from this kind of crime.

2. A popular way to motivate people to spend money is through advertising. Look through some popular American magazines or newspapers to find ads for three different products. Read the ads and determine to whom the advertisers are trying to appeal. Use the following questions to help you:

   • Are there any people in the ad? If there are, what kind of people—young, old, single, professional, etc.?

   • What kinds of words does the ad use to describe the product?

   • What magazine or newspaper did you find it in? Who reads that magazine or newspaper?

   • Do certain words appear in all the ads you found? Which ones?

3. The film *Lost in America*, written and directed by Albert Brooks, is a comedy about the value of money in the United States. Find this videotape in the library or in a video store and watch it. How is the film related to the themes in this chapter?

4. Interview someone who has made a major purchase recently—a car, house, or boat, for example. Ask him or her about the experience. Start with these questions:

   • How did the salesperson treat you?

   • How did it feel to spend so much money?

   • Was it a happy experience?

   Add other questions that interest you.

★★★

A L M A N A C   For additional cultural information, refer to the Almanac on pages 221–234. The Almanac contains lists of useful facts, maps, and other information to enhance your learning.

CHAPTER 3

★★★

Traditions

Every culture has traditions that help define it as a culture. The United States is no different. Although U.S. traditions come from many different cultures, these traditions still have an unmistakable American flavor.

PART ONE

𝕿raditions : Home for the Holidays

Although many American holidays, such as Christmas, are similar to those celebrated in other countries, some are uniquely American. American Thanksgiving, for example, has foods and activities that make it different from other autumn celebrations.

Before You Read

Marcher in a Columbus Day parade

Ten Facts About Columbus Day

1. Columbus Day is celebrated the second Monday in October.

2. Columbus Day honors the anniversary of the landing of Christopher Columbus in the New World.

3. Columbus landed in the Americas on October 12, 1492 while making a voyage to the Indies.

4. Columbus was born in 1451 in Genoa, Italy.

5. Columbus died on May 20, 1506.

6. The first celebration of Columbus Day took place in New York City in 1792.

7. In 1892, the U.S. President issued a proclamation to observe the 400th anniversary of the discovery of the New World.

8. In 1934 President Franklin D. Roosevelt asked that all states observe October 12 as a national holiday.

9. In 1937, there was a proclamation designating Columbus Day.

10. Today, Columbus Day, sometimes called Discovery or Landing Day, is observed in most states.

In the following short reading, the author writes humorously about Columbus Day.

Before you read this piece, think about the following questions:

- When is Columbus Day? What does it celebrate?
- Is there a similar holiday in your home culture?
- Do you think the United States should celebrate Columbus Day?

Cultural Cues

Vikings Explorers from northern Europe; some believe they traveled to North America before Columbus did.

About the Author

Bill Bryson was born in 1951 in Des Moines, Iowa. He grew up there, but has spent most of his adult life in England. His books include *The Penguin Dictionary for Writers and Editors, Mother Tongue: The English Language*, and the travel books *The Lost Continent, Notes from a Small Island* and *A Walk in the Woods*. He is married and has four children, and has recently returned to the United States.

Columbus Day

by Bill Bryson

It was the Columbus Day weekend and the roads were busy. Columbus has always seemed to me an odd choice of hero for a country that celebrates success as America does because he was such a dismal failure. Consider the facts: he made four long voyages to the Americas, but never once realized
5 that he wasn't in Asia and never found anything worthwhile. Every other explorer was coming back with exciting new products like potatoes and tobacco and nylon stockings, and all Columbus found to bring home were some puzzled-looking Indians–and he thought they were Japanese. But perhaps Columbus's most remarkable shortcoming was that he never actually

10 saw the land that was to become the United States. This surprises a lot of people. They imagine him trampling over Florida, saying, "You know, this would make a nice resort." But in fact his voyages were all spent in the Caribbean and bouncing around the swampy, bug-infested coasts of Central America. If you ask me, the Vikings would make far more worthy heroes 15 for America. For one thing, they did actually discover it. On top of that, the Vikings were manly and drank out of skulls and didn't take any crap from anybody. Now *that's* the American way.

Source: Excerpt from *The Lost Continent: Travels in Small-Town America*

Check Your Comprehension

1. Why does the author think that Columbus is an "odd choice" for an American hero?

2. What surprises a lot of people about Columbus, according to Bryson?

3. Why does Bryson think that Vikings would be more "worthy heroes"?

READING

Find out more about **finding and understanding the main idea** by looking in the Reference Guide to Reading Strategies on pages xii–xiv.

Finding and Understanding the Main Idea

In this short, humorous piece, the writer makes a typical argument. That is, he has a main point, and supports it with three main reasons. Restate his main point and his reasons below.

Main point: _____

_____

Reason 1: _____

_____

_____

_____

Reason 2: _____

_____

_____

_____

Reason 3: _____

_____

_____

_____

VOCABULARY
Adjectives with -*ed* and -*ing*

Each of the following verbs can be turned into an adjective by adding either -*ed* or -*ing*. The -*ed* ending is a passive form which usually shows the quality a person or thing feels:

I felt bor<u>ed</u>.

However, an -*ing* ending is an active form which usually shows the quality a person or thing gives to others:

My brother is a bor<u>ing</u> person. He made me feel bor<u>ed</u>.

Use each of these words with an -*ed* and an -*ing*. Write ten sentences showing you understand the meaning of the word, and the meaning of the word endings.

swamp   *infest*   *excite*   *puzzle*   *surprise*

1. _____
2. _____
3. _____
4. _____
5. _____
6. _____
7. _____
8. _____
9. _____
10. _____

THINK ABOUT IT

1. Bryson uses *hyperbole*, extreme exaggeration, to achieve humor. Find three examples of this kind of exaggeration in the reading. Why does exaggeration make something funny?

2. Do you agree with the author that the Vikings "actually" discovered America? Why or why not?

3. Do you have an opinion about Columbus Day? Should it be celebrated? Do you know about any controversy surrounding the holiday? Discuss these questions with your classmates, or write about them in your journal.

Before You Read

In this reading, the author, a famous weatherman, discusses his favorite holiday: Thanksgiving. In fact, many Americans favor this autumn holiday.

Before you read, think about the following questions:

- Do you know how Thanksgiving is celebrated?
- Have you ever celebrated Thanksgiving?
- Is there a similar holiday in your culture?

Recommended Movies About Thanksgiving

Title	Year	Stars
Home for the Holidays	1995	Holly Hunter Robert Downey Jr.
Planes, Trains, & Automobiles	1987	Steve Martin John Candy
Hannah and Her Sisters	1986	Woody Allen Mia Farrow

Map of the American Southeast

Cultural Cues

Dodge   an American-built automobile.

dapple grays   gray spotted horses.

About the Author

Willard Scott was born March 7, 1934, in Alexandria, Virginia. He is a weather reporter on NBC News' "Today" show. He first appeared on the show in March 1980. Mr. Scott was the first Ronald McDonald, the mascot of McDonald's Restaurants. Mr. Scott is a graduate of American University in Washington, DC, with a Bachelor of Arts (B.A.) in philosophy and religion.

Over My River and Through My Wood
Why I Love Thanksgiving

by Willard Scott

"Hurrah for the fun! Is the turkey done?
Hurrah for the pumpkin pie!"
—Lydia Maria Child, "Over the River and Through the Wood"

One of the strongest similarities I have found in all of us Americans is
5 the way we treat holidays. We all love holidays: they give us a reason to abandon routine, to celebrate, and to make memories. What holiday gives us a better chance to do all these things than Thanksgiving! Thanksgiving weekend is for most of us the longest, least interrupted weekend of the year. It is the ideal time for family and friends to come together again. It is
10 also the most purely American of all holidays, because it celebrates the settling of our country by the Pilgrims over 350 years ago.

For me, Thanksgiving conjures up all the things in life that I respond to most strongly and for which I am truly grateful. There is the simple beauty of the earth and the blessed bounty shared at harvest time. There is the
15 satisfaction that comes from working a crop, the wisdom that comes from knowing that if you handle the land with care, it will yield a rich reward. And there is the tradition of the day itself: the return to my family homesteads in the green hills of Maryland and Virginia, the mouthwatering food, and of course the sharing in the holiday rituals.

20 My father tells me that I spent my first Thanksgiving sprawled on the parlor floor of our family friend Mrs. Tyree's home while happily clutching a roasted turkey leg. But my earliest Thanksgiving memories come from my grandparents' old farm a few years later. For as long as I can remember, my grandparents have had a 75-acre farm in the happily named town of

25 Freeland, in the rolling hills of Harford County, Maryland. Although I visit it now only much too infrequently, it was once the center of my life. The farmhouse was an anchor for the family during the dark days of the Second World War. The garden and the chicken coop fed us well. Everyone knows that good food and sentiments of the heart are closely linked. I learned

30 about that union early on—under the apple trees, in the middle of the tomato patch, and especially in my grandfather's smokehouse. The smokehouse was his pride and joy. It was always clean as a whistle and rich with the pungent smells of freshly cured meats. I got my first lessons in dry curing meats the Southern way from my grandfather Scott. When I bought my own

35 farm in Virginia a few years ago, I built a smokehouse for myself!

With food in such abundance and held in such high regard in the Scott household, you can imagine the role the holiday meal played on the farm in Freeland. Nothing evoked the spirit of the holiday like a resounding dinner. It aroused healthy conversation, mended family fences, and made

40 any reason to celebrate doubly special.

I was five years old when I spent my first Thanksgiving at the farm. The year 1939 was historic for many reasons, but for the Scotts it was especially memorable—it was the first time in years we celebrated a wedding in the farmhouse, and it was the only time the house almost became the site of

45 the honeymoon, too! I still remember helping to haul my Aunt Mabel and her new husband to the train station in the middle of an unseasonal snowstorm. Grandfather Scott had planned to rev up his shiny black Dodge and drive the newlyweds to the local train station after dinner, but the moment we bit into our first slice of turkey it started to snow: big wet flakes with lots

50 of sticking power and a wind strong enough to make the snow dance and render windshield wipers useless. "Don't worry," my grandfather said, and we finished the meal. In minutes, everything went—the huge roast turkey, the cooling cranberry sauce, the heavenly clouds of just-whipped potatoes, and our family heirloom pies—the creamy, tangy pumpkin and the deep-

55 dish apple, fragrant with cinnamon and nutmeg. After dinner, my father and grandfather raced to the barn and hitched the two dapple grays to the sleigh. We had a ride I've never forgotten—the entire Scott family and the anxious newlyweds dashing through the snow in a two-horse open sleigh to catch the Honeymoon Express!

60 I like to believe that I can remember clearly every taste, every smell, every slightly off-key note from our player piano—everything except where all the Thanksgivings went. As I grow older, the celebrations seem to merge into one grand set of the best memories. I'll always remember Thanksgivings as the times we ate good food, sang old-fashioned songs, and shared a lot

Source: Excerpt from
The Thanksgiving Book
65   of love with our family and friends. May your Thanksgivings bring you the
same kind of joy.

**Check Your
Comprehension**

1. Why is Thanksgiving such a popular holiday? List five reasons the
author gives in this article.

2. What things is the author thankful for at Thanksgiving time?

3. In your own words, describe the type of life Mr. Scott had as a child.

**READING**

Find out more about
**understanding
descriptions** by
looking in the
Reference Guide to
Reading Strategies on
pages xii–xiv.

Understanding Descriptions

Good descriptions allow us to see, taste, feel, hear, and touch the story, as
if we were part of it. *Concrete* description makes a story come alive. Look
at the examples below:

A beautiful horse	A shiny black horse with a long mane and long, muscular legs
A fun day	A day of playing golf, fishing, and swimming

The difference between the first and second columns is that the second
gives a concrete example that allows the reader to really see what is going
on. "Beautiful" and "fun" are abstract terms that are hard to picture.

Look for passages in the reading that are good examples of concrete
imagery. Find one that appeals to each of the senses. The first one is done
for you. However, find another example of an image that appeals to sight.

sight _shiny black Dodge_ _____

hearing _____

smell _____

taste _____

touch _____

VOCABULARY
Understanding New Vocabulary

Look up these ten words in an English-English dictionary. On another piece of paper, write the definition in your own words. Then, complete the sentences below, showing you understand the meaning of the word.

1. The **bounty** of the season included _____.

2. I tried to **conjure** up _____.

3. A **cranberry** is _____.

4. The most **fragrant** thing I know is _____.

5. We need to **haul** _____.

6. My favorite **heirloom** is _____.

7. A **homestead** is _____.

8. I don't like the **pungent** _____.

9. I received **resounding** _____ because of my _____.

10. You can only use a **sleigh** _____.

THINK ABOUT IT

CNN VIDEO Watch the CNN video on Thanksgiving at the White House. **Discuss these questions:**

1. What is a White House tradition involving the Thanksgiving Day turkey?

2. What does a "presidential pardon" mean for the turkey?

3. What Thanksgiving activities do the President and his family take part in?

1. Why are holidays so important to societies of people?

2. Why does food play an important part of holidays?

3. Willard Scott says, " Everyone knows that good food and sentiments of the heart are closely linked." Do you agree? Give some examples from the story, and from your own experience.

4. What are you thankful for? Write a short essay, explaining what you are thankful for in your life.

PART TWO

Food: Our Daily Bread

American food—hamburgers, French fries, and pizza—has a bad reputation. The readings in this section show, however, that this stereotype is not the whole truth about the American diet.

The Most Popular Snacks in the United States

	Snack	Amount eaten (pounds)	Money spent ($)
1	Potato chips	6.69	17.80
2	Tortilla chips	4.56	11.30
3	Snack nuts	1.71	5.70
4	Pretzels	2.30	4.27
5	Microwave popcorn	1.46	3.07
6	Filled snacks	1.11	2.98
7	Corn chips	.97	2.45
8	Meat snacks	.17	2.10
9	Ready-to-eat popcorn	.64	1.81
10	Party mix	.38	1.12

Source: Adapted from *The Top 10 of Everything* 1996, p. 193. New York: Doring Kindersley, 1995

This reading discusses the unique contribution of American foods to the art of cooking. The author also discusses the contributions of different ethnic groups to what we know as American food.

Before you read, think about the following questions:

* What foods do you think of as being American?
* How has your own culture's cuisine contributed to the American diet?

Jeff Smith has written many cookbooks about American and international food.

Cooking AmeriCan

by Jeff Smith

We Americans have had a bad image of ourselves and our food for a long time, and I am done with it. I am so tired of people from the New World bowing to Europe, particularly France, when it comes to fine eating. We

seem to think that if it comes from Europe it will be good, and if it comes
5 from America it will be inferior. Enough! We really do not understand our
own food history, and I think that means we do not actually understand
our own culture.

Most Americans do not think of themselves as an ethnic group, but we
are an ethnic body, all of us put together. The word *ethnic* comes from the
10 Greek *ethnos*, meaning "nation." It refers not necessarily to a bloodline but
to a group of persons distinguished by singular customs, characteristics,
and language. While we are a nation populated for the most part by immigrants, we are nevertheless an ethnic group, a strange mixture, perhaps,
but an ethnic group. We share a common language, but more importantly
15 we share a common memory. And there certainly is such a thing as American
ethnic cooking. It is cooking that helps us remember and restore that common cultural memory.

All ethnic groups have foods that help them continue to identify themselves. Most of us Americans are not aware of the wonderfully complex
20 history of our own foods since most of us still think that everything here
came over from Europe or some other part of the world. The following is
a list of food products that are ours, coming from one of the Americas, and
these products were unknown in Europe prior to the discovery of the New
World:

25 corn	sweet potatoes	tomatoes
turkey	vanilla beans	avocados
peanuts	potatoes	black walnuts
pimentos	lima beans	kidney beans
allspice	navy beans	bell peppers
30 squashes	pumpkins	string beans
cocoa	wild rice	cranberries

So there! These foods belong to us, and they actually do help define us.
You enjoy turkey at Christmas even though your grandmother was born in
Sicily. And the influence that these foods have had upon the rest of the
35 world should never be overlooked. Italy had no tomatoes, Ireland had no
potatoes, and Switzerland had no vanilla or chocolate. Spain had no bell
peppers or pimentos and China had no corn, peanuts, or sweet potatoes.
These last three edibles kept most of China alive at the beginning of the
century. American foods have influenced the diet of the world.
40 When thinking about who we are we must remember that America was
discovered by Europeans while on the search for food. Columbus was not
after property for housing developments, he was after trade routes for valuable spices! And ever since the Europeans began moving about between the
New World and the Old there has been such a thing as American ethnic food,
45 food that is ours and is foreign to the rest of the planet. You see, I am not
talking about hamburgers and hot dogs, though these are the delicacies that
most Americans use in answering the question about "real American food."

Our real American foods have come from our soil and have been used by many groups—those who already lived here and those who have come here to live. The Native Americans already had developed an interesting cuisine using the abundant foods that were so prevalent.

The influence that the English had upon our national eating habits is easy to see. . . . They were a tough lot, those English, and they ate in a tough manner. They wiped their mouths on the tablecloth, if there happened to be one, and ate until you would expect them to burst. European travelers to this country in those days were most often shocked by American eating habits, which included too much fat and too much salt and too much liquor. Not much has changed! And, the Revolutionists refused to use the fork since it marked them as Europeans. The fork was not absolutely common on the American dinner table until about the time of the Civil War, the 1860s. Those English were a tough lot.

Other immigrant groups added their own touches to the preparation of our New World food products. The groups that come still have a special sense of self-identity through their ancestral heritage, but they see themselves as Americans. This special self-identity through your ancestors who came from other lands was supposed to disappear in this country. The term *melting pot* was first used in reference to America in the late 1700s, so this belief that we would all become the same has been with us for a long time. Thank goodness it has never worked. The various immigrant groups continue to add flavor to the pot, all right, but you can pick out the individual flavors easily.

The largest ancestry group in America is the English. There are more people in America who claim to have come from English blood than there are in England. But is their food English? Thanks be to God, it is not! It is American. The second largest group is the Germans, then the Irish, the Afro-Americans, the French, the Italians, the Scottish, and the Polish. The Mexican and American Indian groups are all smaller than any of the above, though they were the original cooks in this country.

Some unusually creative cooking has come about in this nation because of all those persons that have come here. Out of destitution comes either creativity or starvation, and some of the solutions that the new Americans have come up with are just grand. Only in America would you find an Italian housewife sharing recipes with her neighbor from Ireland. It has always been this way. The Native Americans were gracious enough to teach the first Europeans how to cook what was here, and we have been trading favorite dishes with one another ever since.

I am talking about American food—food that has come to us from the early days, using American products, and that continues to provide one of the best diets on earth. I am not talking contemporary artsy plates, nor am I talking about *nouvelle gauche*. And, I am not talking about meat loaf and lumpy mashed potatoes. Even at the time of the writing of the Declaration of Independence we were celebrating one of the most varied, and probably the best, cuisines in the world. It has not changed.

Source: *The Frugal Gourmet Cooks American*

Check Your Comprehension

1. Why does the author state that all Americans belong to one ethnic group? How is this different from the usual meaning of "ethnic"?

2. Why didn't many Americans use forks before the time of the Civil War?

3. What is meant by the phrase "*melting pot*"?

4. What are the causes of the "unusually creative cooking" that the author says has come from the United States?

VOCABULARY
Using Your First Language

Sometimes context can't give you enough information about a foreign word. Look at this list of food items from the reading and circle any that you aren't sure about. Look them up in a bilingual dictionary, and write the words in your native language.

corn	turkey	peanuts
pimentos	allspice	squashes
cocoa	sweet potatoes	vanilla beans
potatoes	lima beans	navy beans
pumpkins	wild rice	tomatoes
avocados	black walnuts	kidney beans
bell peppers	string beans	cranberries

READING

Find out more about **outlining** by looking in the Reference Guide to Reading Strategies on pages xii–xiv.

Outlining

Using your understanding of the words in the vocabulary exercise, now classify these foods into groups. Use the following outline form.

Foods of the Americas

I. Vegetables

   A. Beans

      1. _____

      2. _____

      3. _____

      4. _____

      5. _____

      6. _____

   B. Peppers

      1. _____

      2. _____

   C. Root vegetables

      1. _____

      2. _____

   D. Gourds

      1. _____

      2. _____

II. Fruits* and Berries

      1. _____

      2. _____

      3. _____

III. Nuts and Spices

   A. Nuts

      1. _____

      2. _____

   B. Spices

      1. _____

IV. Cereals and Grains

      1. _____

      2. _____

V. Meats

      1. _____

*Hint: Two food items are often considered to be vegetables but they are fruits. Avocados are one of these.

THINK ABOUT IT

1. Were you surprised to learn that the list of 21 foods originated in the Americas? Which ones surprised you most?

2. Are any of these 21 foods used regularly in your own culture's cuisine? Which ones?

3. In general, what is your opinion of American food? What specific dishes do you like? What don't you like?

4. Following is a recipe for chocolate chip cookies, probably the most popular type of cookie in the United States. Look at the recipe:

Chocolate Chip Cookies

2¼ cups all-purpose flour

1 teaspoon baking soda

1 teaspoon salt

1 cup (two sticks) softened butter or margarine

¾ cup granulated sugar

¾ cup firmly packed brown sugar

1 teaspoon vanilla extract

2 eggs

1 12-oz package (2 cups) chocolate chips

Preheat oven to 375 degrees Fahrenheit. In a small bowl, combine flour, baking soda and salt; set aside. In a large bowl, combine butter, sugar, brown sugar and vanilla extract; beat until creamy. Add eggs and beat. Gradually add flour mixture; mix well. Stir in chocolate chips. Drop by teaspoonfuls onto ungreased cookie sheets. Bake 8 to 10 minutes. Makes about 50 cookies.

   a. What are the "rules" for writing a recipe? Complete the following statements:

   i. The ingredients are listed (in what order?) _____

   _____

   ii. The instructions use _____ sentences.

   iii. You must include information about these four things:

	Hint:		Hint:
_____	(oven)	_____	(time)
_____	(containers)	_____	(quantity)

   b. What is one of your favorite foods from your own or from American culture? Write a recipe for that dish. Use the same format as the recipe above uses.

   c. Explain to your classmates how to prepare this dish. Distribute copies of your recipe.

d. If you have a kitchen, prepare cookies according to the recipe. Report in writing or to your class how easy (or difficult) it was. Were you successful? Bring samples to the class if you want.

Before You Read

Nutritional Content of McDonald's Burgers & Fries

Item	Calories	Fat (grams)	Protein (grams)
Hamburger	260	9	13
Cheeseburger	320	13	15
Big Mac	560	31	26
Large French Fries	450	22	6
Small Chocolate Shake	360	9	11

Source:
http://www.mcdonalds.com

This reading talks about the history of three fast food restaurants in America. It focuses on Columbus, Ohio, which is considered the fast food capital of the United States.

Before you read, think about these questions:

• Do you enjoy fast food? Which types?

• What is your opinion of the impact of U.S. fast food on the world?

Cultural Cues

Chuck and Di Prince Charles of England, and the late Diana Spencer, his wife.

celeb A shortened version of the word *celebrity*.

Fast Food Becomes High Art in Ohio

Only in the USA do folks wax nostalgic about the burgers, fries and shakes of their youth. And only Columbus, Ohio, elevates those cheesy memories to high art with museum exhibits:

Though Wendy's Old Fashioned Hamburgers dates to just 1969, the
5 Columbus-based chain celebrates its legacy with a sizeable museum/restaurant on the site of the original outlet at 257 E. Broad St. Two dining rooms house interactive kiosks showing award-winning Wendy's commercials, and such memorabilia as the original skillet used to fry the first square burger; the Wendy's Christmas card and tour jacket; the dress made for founder Dave
10 Thomas' daughter Wendy when she posed for the logo; and celeb photos

Source: *USA Today*

galore. Highlight: a shot of Chuck and Di in their royal wedding carriage as they pass a Wendy's in London.

15 White Castle, a 299-unit burger chain headquartered in Columbus, celebrates its 75th birthday with a display this fall at the Ohio Historical Society. The company, founded in 1921 in Wichita, Kansas, is one of the 20 oldest burger chains and is famous for its Slyders or Belly Bombers: square, palm-sized, five-holed, steam-grilled burgers dotted with onions and pickles. The museum display will 25 include items such as old uniforms, menus, photos, mugs, plates and cooking utensils.

On a smaller scale, McDonald's evokes its past with one of its retro-styled McDonald's Classic restaurants at 7190 Sawmill Rd. The tiny outlet 30 with the imposing golden arches is similar to the original founded in 1955 in Des Plains, Illinois. A display case features old-style paper hats worn by employees, paper cups and vintage photos, including one of founder Ray Kroc with the quotation: "It's not what you do but the way that you do it."

Check Your Comprehension

1. What three restaurants feature museums of their histories?

2. What are some of the items shown in the museums?

3. Which is the oldest restaurant mentioned in this article?

 **READING**

Find out more about **scanning** by looking in the Reference Guide to Reading Strategies on pages xii–xiv.

Scanning

Scan the article again and complete the following information about the fast food restaurants mentioned in the article. (Not all the information is available for each restaurant.)

Name of Restaurant	Year Founded	Location of Original Restaurant	Name of Founder	What the Museum Features

VOCABULARY
Words of History

The following words are associated with talking about the past and history. Be sure you understand what they mean.

nostalgia	*old-style*	*evoke*	*retro-style*
founded	*legacy*	*memorabilia*	*vintage*

Answer the following questions, which use these vocabulary items:

1. Describe an event for which you have **nostalgia.**

    _____

    _____

2. Find out when your school was **founded.**

    _____

    _____

3. What kind of food do you prefer: **old-style** or modern?

    _____

    _____

4. What is the most important **legacy** you will leave?

    _____

    _____

5. What memory of your childhood **evokes** happy feelings?

    _____

    _____

6. Do you have any **memorabilia** from an important event in your life? What is it?

    _____

    _____

7. Is there a **vintage** car you like? What is it?

    _____

    _____

THINK ABOUT IT

1. What do you think of the idea of fast food restaurant museums? Why do you think these companies want to open these museums? Would you visit one of them if you visited Columbus, Ohio?

2. Many people object to the effect that fast food restaurants have had on eating habits, cultures, and the environment. What is your opinion?

3. What if you could open a museum that featured you and your life? What objects would you put in it? What photographs would be the most important? Write a description of your museum, including its contents and a timeline of your life.

S Y N T H E S I S

Discussion and Debate

1. There is a common proverb in the United States, "You are what you eat." If this is true, what are you? Are there proverbs in your first language about food? Explain them to your classmates.

2. The Thanksgiving holiday is often called the most typically American holiday—it is not tied to a particular religion, and it features eating and American football. What other holidays do you associate with the United States?

3. The winter holidays—Thanksgiving, Christmas, New Year's Day—are a time of great joy and celebration for most people in the United States However, they are also a time of great stress or depression for many, especially the poor, or the elderly. Why might this be? What could be done to help these groups enjoy the holidays more?

Writing Topics

1. What is your favorite holiday? It can be either an American holiday or one from another culture. In a short essay, describe the holiday, what traditions are associated with it, and why it is special to you.

2. Food and holidays go together. Ask someone about a typical holiday food. Ask what holiday this food is part of, and why it is important. Then, do a little research—find out how you prepare this food. Don't go to a cookbook! Ask someone to explain it, and write down his or her instructions. Write a short report on your findings.

3. Although Christmas is a national holiday in the United States, it is also a Christian holiday. For this reason, many groups do not celebrate Christmas, but another winter holiday. Do you know about any of these other holidays? Research one of these holidays, such as Hannukah or Kwanzaa, and write a short report on it.

4. Write about your first experience eating "typical" American food. What was it like? Did you enjoy it? What did you eat? What type of American food would you like to try? Write about these questions in your journal.

On Your Own

1. What is a food bank? Find out about food banks in your area and report on them to your class. In particular, find out what kinds of donations they accept. (If you can, make a donation to the food bank.)

2. Check your local television listings for programs that give instruction in cooking. Watch one of these programs and report to your class about what you learned.

3. Talk to three people about their eating habits. You may want to use these questions:

   • How many meals do you eat in restaurants in one week?

   • How many times do you shop in a grocery store or market in one week?

   • What is your favorite food?

   • What food do you dislike?

   • Do you think you eat a healthy diet?

   Compare your answers with your classmates' results. What conclusions can you draw?

★★

A L M A N A C   For additional cultural information, refer to the Almanac on pages 221–234. The Almanac contains lists of useful facts, maps, and other information to enhance your learning.

CHAPTER 4

★★

People

Physical appearance, beauty, health, and growing older
are topics that concern Americans greatly. This chapter
looks at some of these issues, and how they affect
the American population.

PART ONE

Beauty: In the Eye of the Beholder

Although no one agrees on the definition of "beauty," it is big business
in the United States. Cosmetic companies, cosmetic surgery,
weight loss programs, weight loss drugs, and beauty contests
are all part of the beauty industry.

Before You Read

Important Dates in Miss America History

1921	The first Miss America Pageant was held.
1935	The Executive Director, Lenora Slaughter, demanded that a talent competition be added.
1940	The competition moved to the Convention Center, Atlantic City, which is still its home today.
1943	The first college student, Jean Bartel of UCLA, was crowned.
1945	The first scholarship was awarded to Bess Myerson, the first Jewish woman and the first college graduate to become Miss America.
1947	Barbara Walker was the last Miss America to be crowned in a swimsuit.
1950s	The Miss America Scholarship Program reached over $250,000.
1954	The first nationally-televised Miss America Pageant was aired. It became the fourth longest-running live event in television history.
1955	Bert Parks began his 25-year career as Master of Ceremonies, making the song "There She Is, Miss America" famous.
1966	The show's move to NBC was also the Pageant's first color broadcast.
1970	Cheryl Brown, Miss Iowa, was the first African-American woman to compete in the national Pageant.
1984	Vanessa Williams became the first African-American Miss America.
1994	Heather Whitestone, who is deaf, was the first woman with a disability to be crowned.
1996	For the first time ever, the American public helped select the contestant who became Miss America. Through a telephone vote, viewers were the "eighth judge" in scoring for the top ten semi-finalists.

Source: http://www.
missamerica.org

In the following reading, the author looks at our attitudes toward appearances, particularly in the area of beauty contests.

Before you read, think about these questions:

- Have you ever seen a beauty contest, such as "Miss America" or "Miss Universe"? What do you think of these contests?
- Do you think we focus too much on beauty as a society? Do you think this is a problem?

Cultural Cues	*Goldie Hawn* An American actor, star of many films, including *The First Wives Club* and *Cactus Flower*

Goldie Hawn An American actor, star of many films, including *The First Wives Club* and *Cactus Flower*

Dick Butkus An American football player who played for the Chicago Bears in the late 1960s and early 1970s

Donald Trump A very wealthy American businessman who owns casinos and hotels in New York and New Jersey

Tom Cruise An American actor, star of many films, including *Jerry Maguire* and *Top Gun*

Tom Hanks An American actor, star of many films including *Apollo 13* and *Forrest Gump*

Al Pacino An American actor, star of many films including *Scent of a Woman* and *Dog Day Afternoon*

Sean Connery A Scottish actor, star of many films, including several James Bond films and *The Name of the Rose, Highlander,* and *Outland*

John F. Kennedy, Jr. President John F. Kennedy's son

Bic pen The most popular brand of pen in the United States

About the Author Dave Barry is a columnist for the *Miami Herald,* and the author of many books of humor, including *Dave Barry Turns Forty* and *Dave Barry Is from Mars and Venus.* His life was also portrayed in the television comedy series, "Dave's World."

Miss Universe contestants

Queen of the Universe

by Dave Barry It's a Thursday afternoon at the Seville Beach Hotel in Miami Beach, and about a dozen tourists have gathered to watch the Most Beautiful Women in the World emerge from the ladies' room. Here comes Miss Estonia! She's tall and blond and thin! Here comes Miss Venezuela! She's tall and blond
5 and thin, too! Here comes Miss Croatia, and . . . my gosh, SHE'S tall and blond and thin! Here comes Miss Australia! She's a chunky redhead!

No, of course Miss Australia is also tall and blond and thin. It turns out that a great many of the Most Beautiful Women in the World are tall and blond, and ALL of them are thin, thin, thin. These women make Goldie
10 Hawn look like Dick Butkus.

They also smile a lot—big, radiant, glossy-lipped, perfect-teeth smiles. It seems to be their automatic reaction to every stimulus. As each woman comes out, a tourist asks if he can pose with her for a photograph; each one smiles and says yes. They're not only the Most Beautiful Women in the
15 World; they're nice! One by one, they stand next to the tourist, towering over him, radiating at the camera. Then they turn gracefully and walk past the two police officers on guard—the officers try not to stare—into the hotel ballroom. There, they resume rehearsing for the big night, eight days from now, when one of them—in front of a worldwide audience estimated

20   at 600 million people, plus Donald Trump—will be crowned Miss Universe.
The Most Beautiful of All!

When you think about it, "beauty" is a weird concept.

Take noses. A nose is basically a lump of flesh with air holes in it. It
enables you to breathe and smell; it also helps protect your eyes. That's
25   what it's for. Yet for some reason, we have decided, as a culture, that if
these flesh lumps have a certain shape, they are attractive; whereas lumps
that do not conform to that shape—despite the fact that they may perform
the same biological functions just as well, or even better—are deemed ugly.
The same is true for eyes, eyebrows, ears, mouths, hair, teeth, necks, chins,
30   shoulders, arms, hands, stomachs, thighs, calves, feet and all the other
observable body parts. For many of us, how well these body parts do their
jobs is secondary; what matters is how closely the parts come to being
whatever arbitrary shape and size is considered, in our culture, to be beautiful. We obsess about this; we agonize endlessly. We spend billions of dollars
35   trying to change ourselves. We dye our hair and pluck our eyebrows and
religiously smear our faces with expensive products designed to make us
look less like ourselves, and more like the "ideal." We pay surgeons to slice
into us, to remove or rearrange perfectly good flesh. We eat, God help us,
rice cakes.

40   Why do we care so much about appearance? Is it some kind of mass
psychosis? Or is it natural? Do other species do the same thing? If a male
squid is clinging to an undersea rock, and two female squids swim past,
does the male look at them and decide which one is more beautiful? Does
he notice the shapes of their beaks, the way the undersea light glints from
45   their skin slime, the size of the suckers on their tentacles; and does he think
to himself, in some squid way, "Well, the one on the left is ugly, but the one
on the right is a BABE"?

We may not know what squids think about beauty, but there is no question
what popular Western culture thinks about it. Watch any TV show; open
50   any magazine; go to any movie. You can't avoid the obvious conclusion:
Popular Western culture thinks beauty is a very, very big deal. Especially
feminine beauty. This is one of the two big reasons why I'm glad I'm a man
(the other one is that I will never be called upon to have an entire human
being pass through one of my bodily orifices).

55   Men definitely get more slack in the beauty department. A man can be
bald, or carry a few dozen extra pounds, or have bad skin or a big nose, and
still be considered attractive. Granted, there's a definite "beauty" standard for
males: the square-jawed male models with rippling abdominals; Tom Cruise;
and of course John F. Kennedy Jr. These men are considered beautiful, and
60   regular men cannot hope to look like them. But regular men CAN look at,
say, Tom Hanks, or Sean Connery without his wig, or Al Pacino—who is a
Registered Sex Object—and say: "Hey, I don't look THAT different."

Regular women can't look at female romantic-lead movie stars, or super-

models, and say this. More and more, it seems, the women who are
65 certified as beautiful look less and less like the vast majority of women. It
is not enough for a woman to have the right cheekbones, the right eyes,
the right mouth, the right nose and flawless skin: Beautiful women, it has
been decided, must also be extraordinarily tall, and they must have no more
body fat than a Bic pen. If you don't meet these criteria, then . . . sorry!
70 You're the ugly squid!

The Miss Universe Pageant, like most pageants, does not formally call
itself a "beauty" pageant. You hear virtually no overt talk from pageant
officials about physical appearance; you hear a LOT of talk about qualities
such as personality, poise, talent, integrity and "inner beauty." I'm not saying
75 that those qualities are totally irrelevant to winning a pageant; I'm just saying
that if you have all of those qualities, plus a Nobel Prize, but you also happen
to have a big nose, or wide hips, or a sagging butt, or the tiniest hint of
cellulite, you have no more chance of becoming Miss Universe than I do.

Source: *Miami Herald*

Check Your Comprehension

1. Why does the author think that beauty is a "weird concept"?

2. Why does the author think that men have it easier than women in the "beauty department"?

3. What is the author's opinion about beauty contests?

 **READING**

Find out more about **finding and understanding the main idea** by looking in the Reference Guide to Reading Strategies on pages xii–xiv.

Finding and Understanding the Main Idea

Although the author writes humorously about his subject, he has a clear argument he wants to make. What is it? Write one sentence below that states the main idea.

_____

_____

_____

For each paragraph, the author also makes a main point. Restate in your own words the author's ten main points (the first one is done for you):

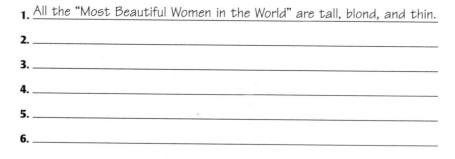

1. All the "Most Beautiful Women in the World" are tall, blond, and thin.

2. _____

3. _____

4. _____

5. _____

6. _____

7. _____

8. _____

9. _____

10 _____

VOCABULARY
Using Prepositions

Read the following sentences and write the correct prepositions in the blanks.

1. A dozen tourists have gathered to watch the Most Beautiful Women _____ the world emerge _____ the ladies' room.

2. A tourist asks if he can pose _____ her _____ a photograph.

3. They stand next to the tourist, towering _____ him, radiating _____ the camera.

4. They resume rehearsing _____ the big night, eight days _____ now.

5. A nose is basically a lump _____ flesh _____ air holes in it.

6. We spend billions _____ dollars trying to change ourselves.

7. Why do we care so much _____ appearance?

8. This is one _____ the two big reasons why I'm glad I'm a man.

THINK ABOUT IT

1. Do you agree with Barry about beauty? Why or why not?

2. The author mentions the fact that plastic surgery is one option that many people take in order to achieve "ideal beauty." What do you think of the practice of plastic surgery? Can you think of any circumstances in which it would be necessary?

3. Have you ever seen a beauty contest on television? What was it like?

4. Are beauty contests popular in your culture? Are they different from what Barry describes? How?

Before You Read

Ideal Weight

Height		Weight in Pounds	
Feet	Inches	Men	Women
4	10	——	102-131
4	11	——	103-134
5	0	——	104-137
5	1	——	106-140
5	2	128-150	108-143
5	3	130-153	111-147
5	4	132-156	114-151
5	5	134-160	117-155
5	6	136-164	120-159
5	7	138-168	123-163
5	8	140-172	126-167
5	9	142-176	129-170
5	10	144-180	132-173
5	11	146-184	135-176
6	0	149-188	138-179
6	1	152-192	——
6	2	155-197	——
6	3	158-202	——
6	4	162-207	——

Source: Metropolitan Life Insurance Company Height and Weight Tables

The author of the following essay discusses weight from an unusual perspective. She uses a lot of descriptive vocabulary that might be unfamiliar; however, try to read the essay the first time without using your dictionary.

Before you read, think about the following questions:

• How are overweight people regarded in your culture?

• Do you think you have any stereotypes about the behavior of overweight people?

• How is overweight defined in your culture?

Cultural Cues

S&H Green Stamps Stamps that were once given for the amount of money spent, that could be traded for merchandise.

About the Author

Suzanne Britt is the author of *Skinny People Are Dull and Crunchy Like Carrots*. She teaches English at Meredith College in North Carolina.

That Lean and Hungry Look

by Suzanne Britt

Caesar was right. Thin people need watching. I've been watching them for most of my adult life, and I don't like what I see. When these narrow fellows spring at me, I quiver to
5 my toes. Thin people come in all personalities, most of them menacing. You've got your "together" thin person, your mechanical thin person, your condescending thin person, your tsk-tsk thin person, your efficiency-expert thin per-
10 son. All of them are dangerous.

In the first place, thin people aren't fun. They don't know how to goof off, at least in the best, fat sense of the word. They've always got to be adoing*. Give them a coffee break,
15 and they'll jog around the block. Supply them with a quiet evening at home, and they'll fix the screen door and lick S & H Green stamps. They say things like "there aren't enough hours in the day." Fat people never say that. Fat
20 people think the day is too damn long already.

Thin people make me tired. They've got speedy little metabolisms that cause them to bustle briskly. They're forever
25 rubbing their bony hands together and eyeing new problems to "tackle." I like to surround myself with sluggish, inert, easygoing fat people, the kind who believe that if you clean it up today, it'll
30 just get dirty again tomorrow.

Some people say the business about the jolly fat person is a myth, that all of us chubbies are neurotic, sick, sad people. I disagree. Fat people may not
35 be chortling all day long, but they're a hell of a lot *nicer* than the wizened and shriveled. Thin people turn surly, mean,

*adoing = doing

and hard at a young age because they never learn the value of a hot-fudge sundae for easing
40 tension. Thin people don't like gooey soft things because they themselves are neither gooey nor soft. They are crunchy and dull, like carrots. They go straight to the heart of the matter while fat people let things stay all blurry
45 and hazy and vague, the way things actually are. Thin people want to face the truth. Fat people know there is no truth. One of my thin friends is always staring at complex, unsolvable problems and saying, "The key thing is. . . ." Fat people never say that. They know
50 there isn't any such thing as the key thing about anything.

Thin people believe in logic. Fat people see all sides. The sides fat people see are rounded
55 blobs, usually gray, always nebulous and truly not worth worrying about. But the thin person

persists. "If you consume more calories than you burn," says one of my thin friends, "you will gain weight. It's that simple." Fat people always grin when they hear statements like that. They know better.

Fat people realize that life is illogical and unfair. They know very well that God is not in his heaven and all is not right with the world. If God was up there, fat people could have two doughnuts and a big orange drink anytime they wanted it.

Thin people have a long list of logical things they are always spouting off to me. They hold up one finger at a time as they reel off these things, so I won't lose track. They speak slowly as if to a young child. The list is long and full of holes. It contains tidbits like "get a grip on yourself," "cigarettes kill," "cholesterol clogs," "fit as a fiddle," "ducks in a row," "organize," and "sound fiscal management." Phrases like that.

They think these 2,000-point plans lead to happiness. Fat people know happiness is elusive at best and even if they could get the kind thin people think about, they wouldn't want it. Wisely, fat people see that such programs are too dull, too hard, too off the mark. They are never better than a whole cheesecake.

Fat people know all about the mystery of life. They are the ones acquainted with the night, with luck, with fat, with playing it by ear. One thin person I know once suggested that we arrange all the parts of a jigsaw puzzle into groups according to size, shape, and color. He figured this would cut the time needed to complete the puzzle by at least 50 percent. I said I wouldn't do it. One, I like to muddle through. Two, what good would it do to finish early? Three, the jigsaw puzzle isn't the important thing. The important thing is the fun of four people (one thin person included) sitting around a card table, working on a jigsaw puzzle. My thin friend had no use for my list. Instead of joining us, he went outside and mulched boxwoods. The three remaining fat people finished the puzzle and made chocolate, double-fudge brownies to celebrate.

The main problem with thin people is that they oppress. Their good intentions, bony torsos, tight ships, neat corners, cerebral machinations, and pat solutions loom like dark clouds over the loose, comfortable, spread-out, soft world of the fat. Long after fat people have removed their coats and shoes and put their feet up on the coffee table, thin people are still sitting on the edge of the sofa, looking neat as a pin, discussing rutabagas. Fat people are heavily into fits of laughter, slapping their thighs and whooping it up, while thin people are still politely waiting for the punch line.

Thin people are downers. They like math and morality and reasoned evaluation of the limitations of human beings. They have their skinny little acts together. They expound, prognose, probe, and prick.

Fat people are convivial. They will like you even if you're irregular and have acne. They will come up with a good reason why you never wrote the great American novel. They will cry in your beer with you. They will put your name in the pot. They will let you off the hook. Fat people will gab, giggle, guffaw, gallumph, and gossip. They are generous, giving, and gallant. They are gluttonous and goodly and great. What you want when you're down is soft and jiggly, not muscled and stable. Fat people know this. Fat people have plenty of room. Fat people will take you in.

Source: *Newsweek*

Check Your Comprehension

1. What qualities does the author seem to value in other people?

2. What "evidence" does the author supply to show that fat people are nicer than thin people?

3. How does the author feel about "truth" and logic"?

READING

Find out more about **scanning** by looking in the Reference Guide to Reading Strategies on pages xii–xiv.

Scanning

The author of this article uses a lot of *description* in order to make her point. However, her arguments are clear. Scan the article again, then use the table below to summarize her argument in favor of overweight people and against thin people. One is done for you as an example.

Overweight people . . .	Thin people . . .
	aren't fun.

VOCABULARY
Adjectives–
Negative and Positive

The adjectives below describe human qualities. Find each word in the reading, and then decide whether the author uses it in a positive way, a negative way, or in a neutral way. Place a **+** in the blank before the word if it is positive, a **–** if it is negative, and a **Ø** if it is neutral. Then, use each word in a sentence, showing you understand its meaning.

_____ *convivial*   _____ *jolly*

_____ *easygoing*   _____ *menacing*

_____ *gallant*   _____ *neurotic*

_____ *gluttonous*   _____ *sluggish*

_____ *gooey*   _____ *surly*

Sentences

1. _____

_____

2. _____

_____

3. _____

_____

4. _____

_____

5. _____

_____

6. _____

_____

7. _____

_____

8. _____

_____

9. _____

_____

10. _____

_____

THINK ABOUT IT

1. Do you agree with the author's opinion about overweight people? Why or why not?

2. Do you think a person's size affects his or her personality? If so, how? If not, why not?

3. What are commonly held ideas about physical groups, such as tall and short people, blond-haired and brown-haired people, brown-eyed and blue-eyed people? Do you this these ideas are generally accurate?

    a. Fill in the following chart with adjectives describing commonly held ideas about tall and short people.

Tall People   **Short People**

_____   _____

_____   _____

_____   _____

_____   _____

_____   _____

_____   _____

b. Do you feel that these typical views of tall and short people are
accurate? Why or why not?

PART TWO

AGE: ONLY AS OLD AS YOU FEEL

People all over the world worry about growing old. In the United States,
where the culture is often seen as youth-oriented, it is a particular concern.
There are many businesses that have grown by
paying attention to the needs of older Americans.

Before You Read

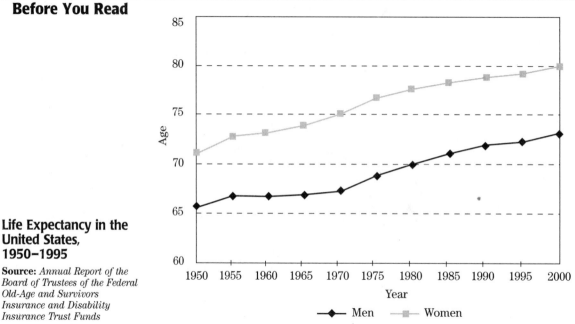

**Life Expectancy in the
United States,
1950–1995**

Source: *Annual Report of the
Board of Trustees of the Federal
Old-Age and Survivors
Insurance and Disability
Insurance Trust Funds*

The author of the following article describes how she feels when her parents
decide to retire and move away.

Before you read, think about the following questions:

- Have your parents or grandparents retired? How did you feel about it?
  How did they feel about it?

- How is retirement treated in your culture? At what age do people
  retire? What do they do after their retirement?

Cultural Cues

L.I. Long Island, a residential island of New York State, near New York City.

Margaret Mead A twentieth-century American anthropologist whose research focused on family and social structures.

I-95 An interstate highway.

About the Author   Randi Kreiss is a writer who lives in New York.

BITTERSWEET FAREWELL OF A GROWN-UP CHILD

by Randi Kreiss

My parents have retired to Florida, and I am suffering an empty nest syndrome. They taught me the value of family, urged me to settle in town, nurtured the love of my children
5 and then they left. I may be 31 years old and a liberated woman, but it still hurts. There are thousands of people like me, experiencing a kind of delayed separation anxiety. Our parents are leaving the old hometown and shaking our
10 roots loose as they go.

In a parody of their ancestors who endured an arduous sea voyage in hopes of a better life, my well-heeled, lively parents tooled down I-95 in search of sunny days and four for bridge.
15 They traded their snow shovels for golf clubs and left us behind to cope with real life.

Part of me is happy for them. Both in their 50's, fit and independent, they have made a gutsy move. Methodically, they lightened their
20 load, sold their house, my father's dental practice, and bought an apartment in Florida.

But somewhere inside, I'm uneasy. Certainly my own life, my husband's life and my children's lives are diminished by their absence.
25 sence. The daily calls or visits or just sightings of my mother's car parked in town were like

touching down for a moment, a warm spot in each day. There were always noncritical ears to hear my side of an argument, a sensible
30 voice to advise compromise. Mainly, the balance they provided on a daily basis is missing, the balance between past and present and the balance between my identity as a child and as a mother. That is all gone, because
35 phone communication is brief and all the news is edited. The daily aches, fears and squabbles are deleted. Good news only, kids, it's Grandma calling.

I wonder about two active people retiring.
40 What will they do for the next 30 or 40 years? Can they really withdraw from the tumult of Northern life and embrace Southern ways? Or are they just exchanging one set of anxieties for another? Perhaps this is self-centered—I
45 may be unwilling to see my parents retire because it is another confirmation that I, too, am getting older.

There is anger in me as well. The child inside her is holding her breath and turning blue; an
50 unreasonable reaction, but let me explain.

We live in a lovely community where people don't grow up longing to find a better life for themselves. They long to be able to afford this one, right here.

55   My parents, sisters, and I lived in our house in Cedarhurst, L.I., for most of our lives. Not that we were overprotected, but I wouldn't sleep at a friend's house until I was 14. When it came time to go "away" to college, I only 60 made it as far as New York University.

Of course, I married the boy I knew in high school, and we settled just down the road in Woodmere. Only my sister threatened our geographic unity. Always the independent one (she 65 made it to Boston for college), she married and settled in Philadelphia.

I began making phone calls to her. "What if you both get a virus in the middle of the night?" I whispered. "What happens when you 70 have a baby and Mom isn't there to help out?"

After three years, they moved just down the road to Hewlett. So there we were, all settled in, reveling in our togetherness, except Mom and Dad, apparently. They smiled lovingly at us 75 all and announced their impending retirement.

I'm the first one to admit it was childlike, but I was angry. My father was always quoting Margaret Mead on the value of an extended family. Now he wanted to deprive his grandchil-80 dren of that experience.

Once the decision was made, my parents began shedding possessions as a dog shakes out fleas. For my husband and me, the house was part of our youth and romance. Memories 85 mixed with the dust and plaster as pictures came down and relics were hauled up from the basement.

We all thought it would be fun to have a garage sale on the last weekend before they 90 moved. Bits and pieces of ourselves, our old life together, were strewn about the garage waiting for buyers. But the day was cold and traffic was slow. By afternoon, my father stood outside alone, handing our things to strangers.

95   Maybe part of the sadness was the air of finality. There were unmentioned but strongly felt parallels to the cleaning out and closing up that accompanies a death. My parents vacuumed up every trace of themselves, and they 100 left town.

The woman in me shouts "bravo" for their daring and the new days before them. They didn't wait for widowhood or illness to force their retirement. They made a free choice.

105   But there is still the child in me, too, perhaps more petulant in this time of adjustment.

Several months ago, the night before my husband and I left for a vacation alone, I heard my 4-year-old daughter crying in bed. She didn't 110 want us to go, she said. Patiently, logically, I explained that mothers and fathers need time away to themselves. She nodded her head, endured my explanation and asked, "But who will be my mother when you're gone?"

115   When we said goodbye to my parents, the child in me was asking the same question.

Source: The *New York Times*

Check Your Comprehension

1. Describe the author's relationship with her parents.

2. Why is the author upset that her parents are moving to Florida?

3. What passages in this reading tell you that the author may have been overprotected by her parents?

 **READING**

Find out more about **understanding intention** by looking in the Reference Guide to Reading Strategies on pages xii–xiv.

Understanding Intention

Most authors write because they want to teach their audience something new, or they want to introduce the readers to a point of view they might not have considered. Why do you think Kreiss wrote this story about her parents? What point of view was she trying to teach us about?

VOCABULARY
Defining Words from Context

Write explanations or definitions of the phrases in italics. These are taken from the reading. Use the information from the passage to help you understand the meaning of the word.

1. My parents have retired to Florida, and I am suffering an *empty nest syndrome.* _____

    _____

2. In a *parody* of their ancestors who endured an arduous sea voyage in hopes of a better life, my *well-heeled,* lively parents *tooled down* I-95 in search of sunny days and *four for bridge.*

    parody _____

    _____

    well-heeled _____

    _____

    tooled down _____

    _____

    four for bridge _____

    _____

3. The daily calls or visits or just sightings of my mother's car parked in town were like *touching down* for a moment, a warm spot in each day.

    _____

    _____

4. Memories mixed with the dust and plaster as pictures came down and *relics* were hauled up from the basement.

    _____

    _____

5. But there is still the child in me, too, perhaps more *petulant* in this
time of adjustment.

_____

_____

THINK ABOUT IT

1. The author describes her feelings about her parents moving away. Is
this different from the way parents feel when their children leave
home? Why or why not?

2. The author emphasizes several times that her feelings are "childish."
Do you agree? Why or why not?

3. Imagine that you are the author's parents. Write a letter to your
daughter explaining why you are moving to Florida. Discuss this with
your classmates before writing the letter if you aren't sure why her
parents moved.

Before You Read

This reading is different than the
others in the book so far. However,
although this is a poem, it is a *narrative*, that is, it tells a story. As you
read the poem, be sure that you ask
yourself the following:

• Who is telling the story?
• Who are the characters?
• What are the events?

Senior citizens

Cultural Cues

The Pearl A book by American author, John Steinbeck

Ladies of the Blessed Trinity A reference to a women's church organization; the church's name is "Blessed Trinity."

Marconi Inventor of the radio

Bon Marché A department store popular in the Pacific Northwest

About the Author Christopher Jane Corkery is a poet whose poems have appeared in the *Atlantic Monthly*. She wrote the book *Blessings* in 1985.

Central and Main

**by Christopher
Jane Corkery**

The little old woman
(she is just that),
whose skin is pale,
yellow from lack
5 of love, of sun
(from age, in short),
who's wrapped in plaid
her mother wore,
has crossed the street
10 to the library's door.

She brings back *The Pearl*
(pleasure for princes!),
which her sister translated
decades ago,
15 but also has under
her elbow the news-
letter of the Ladies
of The Blessed Trinity.
She knows how death
20 has brought two
to their knees today
and knows, without
an allegory,
what comfort, little,
25 can be given.

The other woman
who has crossed at the same
time is alert
to other signals.
30 Her lips are the color
of plum flesh,
her skirt the gauze
of moth wings,
her blouse shines
35 and through it the supple
swing of her breasts

makes red rise up
the throat of Mr.
Wilson, at the corner,
40 who also crosses,
who also dreams,
who loses his purpose
near the Bon Marché.

Now bright cars mosey
45 through the intersection,
of Central and Main,
having stopped for him,
for her, and even
for the old woman.
50 The fall air
is bracing, the sun
is full gold,
yet each one knows,
somehow, what's blowing,
55 brewing, coming.
O life, says each—
three spirits receptive
as Marconi's first
continent-kissing waves—
60 O life,
let it be *me*
who's here forever!

Source: The *Atlantic Monthly*

Check your Comprehension

1. In your own words, write descriptions of the three characters in the poem:

The little old woman _____

_____

_____

The other woman _____

_____

_____

Mr. Wilson _____

_____

_____

2. What do the lines "She knows how death/has brought two/to their knees today" mean?

3. What do the lines "yet each one knows/somehow/what's blowing,/ brewing, coming" mean?

READING

Find out more about **reading aloud** by looking in the Reference Guide to Reading Strategies on pages xii–xiv.

Reading Aloud

Poetry is often easier to understand when it is read aloud. When you read a poem aloud, you hear the rhythm, the rhyme, and the sounds that the author created, all of which contribute to a poem's effect.

Practice reading "Central and Main" aloud. If you have problems with pronunciation of any of the words or phrases, check with your instructor or with a classmate.

VOCABULARY
In Context

In the following table there are four boxes representing four categories of words. The words below are words associated with these categories. Write each word in the correct box. The first one is done for you.

breast	*library*	*throat*
decade	*plum*	~~*yellow*~~
elbow	*skin*	
forever	*the Bon Marché*	

1. colors
  yellow

2. measures of time

3. body parts

4. buildings

THINK ABOUT IT

 Watch the CNN video on the aging population.

Discuss these questions:

1. Who are "baby boomers"?

2. What main problem will baby boomers face at age 65?

3. How are many baby boomers preparing for the future?

1. In your opinion, why does the author name the man, but not the women in this poem?

2. Poems are known for containing *symbols*, concrete objects that symbolize an abstract idea. For example, the "plaid her mother wore" might be a symbol in this poem of age and connection to a family gone. What other symbols can you identify? What might they mean?

3. Do you enjoy reading poetry? Do you have a favorite poet?

4. Have you ever tried to write a poem? Did you enjoy it?

S Y N T H E S I S

Discussion and Debate

1. Some people say that age is superficial or unimportant. They say that it's important to know the "real" person inside. Do you agree? Why or why not?

2. In general, in the United States, it is considered inappropriate to ask an adult how old he or she is, or how much he or she weighs. Are there any taboo questions in your culture?

3. Think of another question to ask one of your classmates about the ideas and opinions presented in this chapter.

Writing Topics

1. If it were easy to change something about yourself—name, age, height, etc.—would you do so? Why or why not? Write about this topic in your journal.

2. Many people believe that certain "handicaps" make you a better person. For example, Suzanne Britt thinks being overweight makes you more fun and sympathetic. Have you (or someone you know) had some kind of "handicap"? Write in your journal about how this "handicap" affected your (or your friend's) life.

3. Write a short essay describing the "perfect" person. Include his or her age, weight, and other details. If such a person existed, do you think you would want to be his or her friend?

On Your Own

1. Look through some magazines for advertisements that include human models. Try to find at least four different types of models—for

example, a heavy person, an old person, a short person, and a child. Respond to the following questions:

a. Describe the age, race, and weight of the models.

b. What products are the models advertising?

c. How are the models dressed?

d. What is the model doing in the ad? Do the advertisements you found reinforce stereotypes about certain types of people? What else can you say about the advertisements?

2. The following films deal with some of the topics in this chapter. Find one in a library or a video store and watch it.

Fatso   *Cocoon*

Babycakes   *Grumpy Old Men*

Harold and Maude   *Driving Miss Daisy*

Big

What was your opinion of the film you watched? Summarize it briefly and give your classmates a review. Include the following information:

a. Who starred in the film?

b. Do you think the actors were good?

c. What did you think of the story? Was it realistic? Funny? Shocking?

d. Would you recommend the film to your friends?

3. Interview five people about the following questions.

a. What is your nationality?

b. Have you ever lied about your age?

c. Have you ever lied about your weight?

d. Do you know anyone who has had plastic surgery?

e. Do you enjoy beauty contests?

f. Have you ever gone on a diet to lose weight?

Compare your answers with your classmates' answers. Try to draw some conclusions about your findings.

★★★

A L M A N A C   For additional cultural information, refer to the Almanac on pages 221–234. The Almanac contains lists of useful facts, maps, and other information to enhance your learning.

★★★

CHAPTER 5

Geography

The United States is a large place. It is known for its diversity of people, history, and landscape. This chapter looks at some of these geographical differences, and the effect these differences have on its people.

PART ONE

Regions: States of Mind

Even though the United States is one country, its separate regions have very
different characteristics. These differences affect the way the language
is spoken, the ethnic make up, and the political and religious views
of the people of each region.

Before You Read

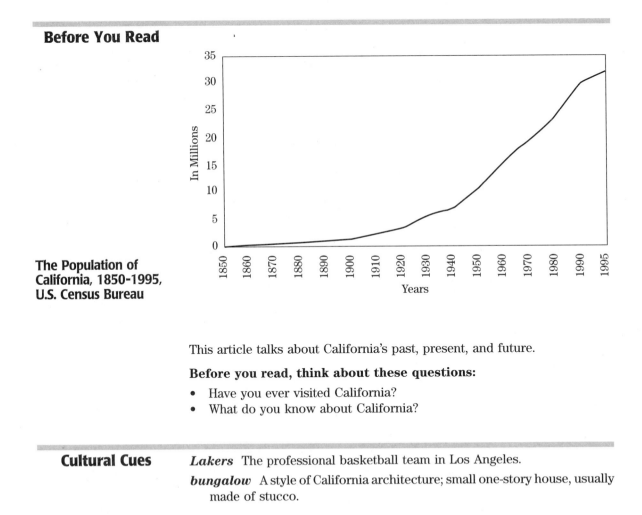

**The Population of
California, 1850-1995,
U.S. Census Bureau**

This article talks about California's past, present, and future.

Before you read, think about these questions:

* Have you ever visited California?
* What do you know about California?

Cultural Cues

Lakers The professional basketball team in Los Angeles.

bungalow A style of California architecture; small one-story house, usually
made of stucco.

About the Author   Charlie Stoddard graduated from Claremont McKenna College in 1994 and
wrote this editorial for the *Los Angeles Times.* She now lives and works in
Southern California.

An Age of Limits and Definitions

**by Charlie
Stoddard**

Two weeks ago, I left college behind to traverse Los Angeles in an exhausting
search for a place to live. For the better part of daylight, I ricocheted
throughout Santa Monica, bouncing from address to address, hoping to find
the ideal apartment. Eventually I hoped to find *any* apartment, as building
5 after building was eliminated: earthquake damage, too small, too dingy,
olive-green shag carpeting. Building eliminations soon led to neighborhood
and then regional exclusions: The area looked too run-down, "suspicious"
cars drove by just a little too slowly, shady characters hung around outside
the local supermarket. It occurred to me that the California in which I grew
10 up was a California not available to most people; in fact, it was a California
not now available to me.

Exhausted and depressed, I turned a corner to consult my map and
found myself in a neighborhood not unlike my hometown of Claremont:
quaint bungalows, mowed lawns, palms, and picket fences. Now this was
15 California—the California that exists in many people's minds and the California that existed in my reality, the California ideal, the California of my
expectations. The options looked brighter and I continued my search with
renewed vigor. But this vigor was not to last long. There was not an apartment
building to be found, and the cost of the occasional duplex made me reel.
20 Nothing to rent, lease, or even buy within this housing oasis. There was no
room in this area for those with only aspirations of upward mobility and
certainly no room for those with no such ambition. Living within the environment of the California ideal in which I grew up is no longer an expectation,
but part of a dream.

25 California's history comprises the dream, by arrivals from all directions,
of people seeking a better quality of life for themselves and their families.
But that quality has become more difficult to attain, and many of those who
have achieved it now believe they must escape just to maintain it. Those
of us who can afford to now seem to perpetually run from those now
30 following the same California vision that allowed our own success. We
form exclusive communities, without looking back, hoping never to catch
a glimpse of the reality that would require us to see these communities as
the anachronism that they are rapidly becoming.

The reality of California occupies more than the occasional glimpse that
35 we catch on our way to the airport or the Laker game, when we step outside

our sheltered bubble. The reality of California is not the microcosm of palms and bungalows. The reality of California is what we try to escape. That escape is what keeps the California ideal from becoming a reality.

40   Rather than define ourselves according to a dream available only to the few, we need to include in our definition characteristics that make all aspects of California and Californians unique: our ability to adapt to the constant and unexpected changes in our definition; our ability to rumble, roll, shift, and shake without warning and still manage to come out standing. It is this resilience that defines California, a resilience on which we have always 45 stood and on which we should continue to rely.

With the taste of graduation still lingering and the scent of the working world wafting in a bit too quickly, I set out with a new vision of California. For me, it is no longer a leisurely ride down tree-lined streets toward the park and not yet a frenzied commute down crowded highways toward corporate headquarters. While many people see mine as an age of limitless 50 options, it is also a time in which seeking limits and definitions is the most important option.

I now set off to define what it means to be a Californian. I may not get my own bungalow; more likely, a studio in a multi-unit apartment complex. But maybe I'll have a palm outside my window.

Source: *Los Angeles Times*

Check Your Comprehension

1. According to the author, what has happened to the California dream?

2. What did the author's search for an apartment teach her about California?

3. Is the ending of the essay optimistic or pessimistic about the future?

4. What does the author refer to in the passage that says "our ability to rumble, roll, shift, and shake without warning and still manage to come out standing"?

READING

Making Inferences

Find out more about **making inferences** by looking in the Reference Guide to Reading Strategies on pages xii–xiv.

The author of this essay makes many statements that call for inferences. *Inferences* are conclusions you can draw from reading. These require "reading between the lines" for information that isn't stated directly.

For example, the author writes: "earthquake damage, too small, too dingy, olive-green shag carpeting" She doesn't state what her opinion of "olive-green shag carpeting" is, but what *inference* can you draw? Why do you draw that conclusion?

In the following chart write the inferences you can draw from the quotations.

Discuss your results with your classmates. You might have different answers.

Quotation/Question	Inference
1. "earthquake damage, too small, too dingy, olive-green shag carpeting" **Question:** How does she feel about the carpeting?	*She doesn't like this carpeting, because she puts it in the same list as "earthquake damage, too small, too dingy".*
2. "the California ideal with which I grew up is no longer an expectation, but part of a dream." **Question:** What kind of background does the author come from?	
3. "Those of us who can afford to now seem to perpetually run from those now following the same California vision that allowed our own success." **Question:** Who are "those of us" and who are "those now following the same California vision"?	
4. "While many see mine as an age of limitless options . . ." **Question:** What "age" is she referring to, and what "options" is she talking about?	
5. "We form exclusive communities [which are an] anachronism . . ." **Question:** How does the author feel about these communities?	

VOCABULARY
Recognizing Synonyms

In this reading, the author sometimes uses synonyms, or pairs of words that mean the same thing. These synonyms can help you understand the meaning of the word(s) without looking them up.

In the following passages from the reading, circle the synonyms. Then, define what they mean. The first one is done as an example.

1. I (ricocheted) throughout Santa Monica, (bouncing) from address to address.

   Definition: _"To ricochet" means to bounce off of something._

2. Building eliminations soon led to neighborhood and then regional exclusions.

   Definition: _____

3. The area looked too run-down, "suspicious" cars drove by just a little too slowly, shady characters hung around outside the local supermarket.

   Definition: _____

4. There was no room in this area for those with only aspirations of upward mobility. Living within the environment of the California ideal is part of a dream.

   Definition: _____

5. That quality has become more difficult to attain, and many of those who have achieved it now believe they must escape.

   Definition: _____

THINK ABOUT IT

1. What do you think of when you imagine California?

2. What does the author mean by "Those of us who can afford to now seem to perpetually run from those now following the same California vision that allowed our own success"?

3. What problems does the author notice in her home state? How has the author's experience changed her?

Before You Read

Texas Facts

1995 population: 18,723,991

Size: Second largest state in size and population

Total area: 268,601 sq. miles

Capital: Austin

Joined the United States: December 1845, the 28th State

Watch the CNN video on the Guthrie family. **Discuss these questions.**

1. Who is the Guthrie family?

2. What are the Guthries known for?

3. Why are they all gathered together?

In the next reading, the author describes life in a Texas oil town in the early 1920s.

Before you read, think about the following questions:

- What are your impressions of Texas?
- What is a well-known natural resource of Texas?

Cultural Cues

gunny sack A large bag made of burlap, primarily used for storing and shipping grain.

About the Author

The next reading was written in 1943 by a famous folksinger, Woody Guthrie. Woodrow Wilson Guthrie (1912–1967) is best known for his songwriting and singing. However, he also wrote about his experiences as a boy in Texas, in *Bound for Glory*, from which this reading came.

Before you read, you should note that because Guthrie writes in the language of the local people and region, some verbs and pronouns will not look correct to you.

Boy in Search of Something

by Woody Guthrie

I got a letter twice a week as regular as a clock from Pap out on the Texas plains. I told him everything I thought and he told me everything he was hoping. Then, one day, he wrote that his burns had healed up enough for him to go to work, and he'd got him a job managing a whole block of
5   property in Pampa, Texas.

In three days I was standing in the little office shaking his hand, talking old times, and all about my job with him as general handyman around the property. I was just past my seventeenth birthday.

Pampa was a Texas oil boom town and wilder than a woodchuck. It
10   traveled fast and traveled light. Oil boom towns come that way and they go that way. Houses aren't built to last very long, because the big majority of the working folks will walk into town, work like a horse for a while, put the oil wells in, drill the holes down fifteen thousand feet, bring in the black

gushers, case off the hot flow, cap the high pressure, put valves on them,
15 get the oil to flowing steady and easy into the rich people's tanks, and then
the field, a big thick forest of drilling rigs, just sets there pumping oil all
over the world to run limousines, factories, war machines, and fast trains.
There's not much work left to do in the oilfields once the boys have developed
it by hard work and hot sweat, and so they move along down the road, as
20 broke, as down and out, as tough, as hard hitting, as hard working, as the
day they come to town.

The town was mainly a scattering of little old shacks. They was build
to last a few months; built out of old rotten boards, flattened oil barrels,
buckets, sheet iron, crates of all kinds, and gunny sacks. Some were lucky
25 enough to have a floor, others just the dusty old dirt. The rent was high on
these shacks. A common practice was five dollars a week for a three roomer.
That meant one room cut three ways.

Women folks worked hard trying to make their little shacks look like
something, but with the dry weather, hot sun, high wind, and the dust piling
30 in, they could clean and wipe and mop and scrub their shanty twenty-four
hours a day and never get caught up. Their floors always was warped and
crooked. The old linoleum rugs had raised six families and put eighteen
kids through school. The walls were made out of thin boards, one inch thick
and covered over with whatever the women could nail on them: old blue
35 wallpaper, wrapping paper from the boxcars along the tracks, once in a
while a layer of beaver board painted with whitewash, or some haywire
color ranging from deep-sea blue through all of the midnight blues to a
blazing red that would drive a Jersey bull crazy. Each family usually nailed
together some sort of a chair or bench out of junk materials and left it in
40 the house when they moved away, so that after an even thirty-five cents
worth of hand-made wash benches, or an old chair, or table had been left
behind, the landlord hired a sign painter to write the word "Furnished" on
the "For Rent" sign.

Lots of folks in the oil fields come in from the country. They heard about
45 the high wages and the great number of jobs. The old farm has dried up
and blowed away. The chickens are gone dry and the cows have quit laying.
The wind has got high and the sky is black with dust. Blow flies are taking
the place over, licking off the milk pails, falling into the cream, getting hung
up in the molasses. Besides that, they ain't no more work to do on the farm;
50 can't buy no seed for planting, nor feed for the horses and cows.

Source: Excerpt from
Bound for Glory

Check Your Comprehension

1. Why did the author go to Pampa, Texas?

2. Why are the houses built poorly in a "boom town," according to the author?

3. Why is it difficult to keep a house neat in an oil town?

4. Why do people leave the farm to work in the oil fields?

READING

Find out more about **understanding dialect** by looking in the Reference Guide to Reading Strategies on pages xii–xiv.

Understanding Dialect

Woody Guthrie's memoir is written in a regional **dialect.** That is, the written language reflects the way it is actually spoken. Look at the sentences below and rewrite them in standard English.

1. He'd got him a job managing a whole block of property in Pampa, Texas.

   _____

2. They was build to last a few months.

   _____

3. Their floors always was warped and crooked.

   _____

4. The old farm has dried up and blowed away.

   _____

5. Besides that, they ain't no more work to do on the farm.

   _____

Would something be lost in this reading if the author wrote in standard English?

VOCABULARY
Professional Terms

This essay is about work in the oil fields, and so it includes vocabulary specific to work in a particular career. Usually, this kind of vocabulary is most important to those who work in that field, and less important to those who don't. Can you identify the "oil field" vocabulary that the author uses? List the words, and try to guess what they mean. The first one is done for you.

1. *gusher* Oil that shoots up from the ground. _____

2. _____

3. _____

4. _____

5. _____

6. _____

THINK ABOUT IT

1. Guthrie describes what it was like to work in the oil fields of Texas. However, he also makes a comment about the social conditions. What does he think about the conditions of the oil workers? What passage from the text tells you this?

2. What does "The chickens are gone dry and the cows have quit laying" mean?

3. If you are familiar with the television show "Dallas," how does this reading compare to the image of Texas in the television show?

PART TWO

Lifestyles: Country Mice and City Mice

A hundred years ago, most Americans lived in the country, on farms.
Today, the vast majority live in cities. Changes in employment opportunities have
caused this shift in population. However, the different characters of "country people"
and "city people" are still part of the national heritage.

Before You Read

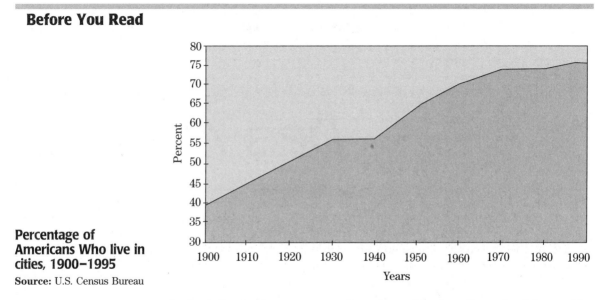

Percentage of Americans Who live in cities, 1900–1995

Source: U.S. Census Bureau

In the following humorous reading, the author describes what life was like growing up in a small city in Iowa. He uses hyperbole—extreme exaggeration—to illustrate what life was like there.

Before you read, think about the following questions:

- Are you from a small town or a big city? What was it like growing up there?

- How do city people feel about country people in your culture?

Cultural Cues

Firestone A tire manufacturing company located in Des Moines, Iowa.

Jack Kerouac A twentieth-century American writer, most famous for a book titled *On the Road*.

105

Viewmaster A device with which you can look at photographic transparencies which has two eyepieces, so that when you look through it, the image appears to be three-dimensional.

Herbert Hoover The thirty-first president of the United States, born in Iowa in 1874.

John Deere The name of a manufacturing company that makes tractors and other farm machinery.

Playboy A magazine known for featuring pictures of nude women.

3D Three-dimensional.

About the Author Bill Bryson is a writer from Iowa who lived in England for many years. He is the author of the book *The Mother Tongue: English and How it Got That Way.*

Fat Girls in Des Moines

by Bill Bryson

I come from Des Moines. Somebody had to. When you come from Des Moines you either accept the fact without question and settle down with a local girl named Bobbi and get a
5 job at the Firestone factory and live there forever and ever, or you spend your adolescence moaning at length about what a dump it is and how you can't wait to get out, and then you settle down with a local girl named Bobbi and
10 get a job at the Firestone factory and live there forever and ever.

Hardly anyone leaves. This is because Des Moines is the most powerful hypnotic known to man. Outside town there is a big sign that
15 says: WELCOME TO DES MOINES. THIS IS WHAT DEATH IS LIKE. There isn't really. I just made that up. But the place does get a grip on you. People who have nothing to do with Des Moines drive in off the interstate, looking
20 for gas or hamburgers, and stay forever. There's a New Jersey couple up the street from my parents' house whom you see wandering around from time to time looking faintly puzzled but strangely serene. Everybody in Des
25 Moines is strangely serene.

When I was growing up I used to think that the best thing about coming from Des Moines was that it meant you didn't come from anywhere else in Iowa. By Iowa standards, Des
30 Moines is a Mecca of cosmopolitanism, a dynamic hub of wealth and education, where people wear three-piece suits and dark socks, often simultaneously. During the annual state high school basketball tournament, when the hay-
35 seeds from out in the state would flood into the city for a week, we used to accost them downtown and snidely offer to show them how to ride an escalator or negotiate a revolving door. This wasn't always so far from reality.
40 My friend Stan, when he was about sixteen,

had to go and stay with his cousin in some remote, dusty hamlet called Dog Water or Dunceville or some such improbable spot—the kind of place where if a dog gets run over by a truck everybody goes out to have a look at it. By the second week, delirious with boredom, Stan insisted that he and his cousin drive the fifty miles into the county town, Hooterville, and find something to do. They went bowling at an alley with warped lanes and chipped balls and afterwards had a chocolate soda and looked at a *Playboy* in a drugstore, and on the way home the cousin sighed with immense satisfaction and said, "Gee, thanks Stan. That was the best time I ever had in my whole life!" It's true.

I had to drive to Minneapolis once, and I went on a back road just to see the country. But there was nothing to see. It's just flat and hot, and full of corn and soybeans and hogs. I remember one long shimmering stretch where I could see a couple of miles down the highway and there was a brown dot beside the road. As I got closer I saw it was a man sitting on a box by his front yard in some six-house town with a name like Spiggot or Urinal, watching my approach with inordinate interest. He watched

me zip past and in the rearview mirror I could see him still watching me going on down the road until at last I disappeared into a heat haze. The whole thing must have taken about five minutes. I wouldn't be surprised if even now he thinks of me from time to time.

He was wearing a baseball cap. You can always spot an Iowa man because he is wearing a baseball cap advertising John Deere or a feed company, and because the back of his neck has been lasered into deep crevasses by years of driving a John Deere tractor back and forth in a blazing sun. (This does not do his mind a whole lot of good either.) His other distinguishing feature is that he looks ridiculous when he takes off his shirt because his neck and arms are chocolate brown and his torso is as white as a sow's belly. In Iowa it is called a farmer's tan and it is, I believe, a badge of distinction.

Iowa women are almost always sensationally overweight—you see them at Merle Hay Mall in Des Moines on Saturdays, clammy and meaty in their shorts and halter-tops, looking a little like elephants dressed in children's clothing, yelling at their kids, calling names like Dwayne and Shauna. Jack Kerouac, of all people, thought that Iowa women were the prettiest in the country, but I don't think he ever went to Merle Hay Mall on a Saturday.

I don't think I would have stayed in Iowa. I never really felt at home there, even when I was small. In about 1957, my grandparents gave me a Viewmaster for my birthday and a packet of discs with the title "Iowa—Our Glorious State." I can remember thinking, even then, that the selection of glories was a trifle on the thin side. With no natural features of note, no national parks or battlefields or

famous birthplaces, the Viewmaster people had
115 to stretch their creative 3D talents to the full.
Putting the Viewmaster to your eyes and clicking the white handle gave you, as I recall, a
shot of Herbert Hoover's birthplace, impres-
sively three-dimensional, followed by Iowa's
120 other great treasure, the Little Brown Church
in the Vale (which inspired the song whose
tune nobody ever quite knows), the highway
bridge over the Mississippi River at Davenport
(all the cars seemed to be hurrying towards
125 Illinois), a field of waving corn, the bridge over
the Missouri River at Council Bluffs and the
Little Brown Church in the Vale again, taken
from another angle. I can remember thinking
even then that there must be more to life than
130 that.

Source: Excerpted from "Fat Girls in Des Moines"

Check Your Comprehension

1. Why doesn't anyone leave Des Moines, according to Bryson?

2. How does Bryson describe Iowans who are not from Des Moines?

3. Why didn't Bryson ever feel at home in Iowa?

4. What were the "glories" of Iowa? Why didn't they seem glorious to Bryson?

 **READING**

Find out more about **understanding humor** by looking in the Reference Guide to Reading Strategies on pages xii–xiv.

Understanding Humor

Hyperbole (pronounced *hi-PER-bo-lee*) means extreme exaggeration. Hyperbole is often used to create humor in writing. It is important to be able to distinguish hyperbole from fact when reading a piece of writing. If you can't tell the difference, it can lead to serious misunderstanding.

Here are some statements from the reading. Check whether they are hyperbole or "true." Then, find three more examples of hyperbole and add them to the list. The first one is done for you.

Statement	Hyperbole	True
1. "Des Moines is the most powerful hypnotic known to man."	X	
2. . . . "the kind of place where if a dog gets run over . . . everybody goes out to have a look at it."		
3. "I come from Des Moines. Somebody had to."		
4. "Iowa women are almost always sensationally overweight."		
5.		X

Statement	Hyperbole	True
6.	X	
7.		X

Before You Read

In this reading, the author talks about a cultural landmark in New York City, the Coney Island amusement park. The author wrote this piece in response to a plan to destroy the Coney Island amusement park and replace it with a more modern attraction.

As you read, think about the following questions:

- Have you ever visited an amusement park? What was it like? Did you enjoy it?
- Have you been to New York City or to Coney Island?

Carousel at Coney Island

Cultural Cues

Ferris wheel An amusement park ride which is a large wheel with seats on it; the wheel rotates, and the riders can look down from a very high distance.

Nathan's cheese fries French fries covered with melted cheese from Nathan's Delicatessen.

sideshow A part of a circus or carnival that featured unusual people; in older times, these might have included people with certain characteristics, such as Siamese twins, or women with beards. Currently, such sideshows are considered unkind and are uncommon. If they do exist, they are likely to feature animal oddities, such as two-headed snakes.

Siamese twins Twins that are born joined together; the term "Siamese twins" is not typically used any longer; "joined twins" is preferable.

About the Author   Steve Zeitlin is the director of City Lore, a New York folklore center.

The Land of Stories and Memories
Coney Island

by Steve Zeitlin   Coney Island is among New York City's "cultural wetlands," urban sites that need to be preserved and nourished as a result of the confluence of history and geography. The Ferris wheels and observation towers on Coney were seen by turn-of-the-century immigrants before they ever gazed on the Statue

5   of Liberty. Through its long line of amusements and sideshows, generations of children had their first roller coaster ride or brush with the bizarre.

    The preservationist James Marston Fitch argues that the value of a place is defined not by dollars and cents but by the quantifiable human energy that was put into it. That energy is more than just construction materials

10   and labor. It consists, too, of all that happened within—the stories, customs and memories that adhere, generation after generation.

    Memories and stories are layered on Coney Island. The site of the proposed Sportsplex is the very place where the Steeplechase amusement park's outrageous Blow Hole Theater (later dubbed the Insanitarium) blew jets of

15   air through grates and sent women's dresses billowing up around their ears. Some women knew about the attraction and held onto their skirts, but little Angelo Brienza, the four-foot-tall clown, prodded them with an electric rod.

    And tales are still told about Steeplechase's founder, George Tilyou, who got his start selling boxes of "Coney Island sand" to tourists. When a fire

20   razed the park in 1907, he put up a sign that read: "I have troubles today that I did not have yesterday, I had troubles yesterday that I have not today. On this site will be erected shortly a better, bigger, greater Steeplechase Park. Admission to the burning ruins—10 cents."

    Leo Wollman, for years the official doctor at Steeplechase, passed on

25   the tale of Sultan, a lion that emerged from the fire that destroyed Dreamland Park in 1911. The lion broke from the flames that engulfed Colonel Ferrari's

Animal House, lunged to the top of the scenic railroad with its mane on fire and died in a hail of police bullets.

30   Wollman also recalled when a patient from the sideshows came into his office and said, "I burned my sister." He answered, "So bring your sister in." She then lifted her dress and there was her sister, a Siamese twin.

I was listening to tapes of oral histories of the park recently when my daughter exclaimed, "They're not going to destroy the old Coney Island, are they?"

35   "Old Coney Island?" I answered. "You're only 12 years old. What do you mean by the old Coney Island?" She described eating Nathan's cheese fries and seeing the contortionist put himself through a clothes hanger at Sideshows by the Seashore a few years ago. For a new generation of children, many black and Latino, it's still the beach, it's still an amusement center.

40   The thrills still churn to memories.

These recollections figure into the value of the place. An amusement area (like the plan the developer Horace Bullard first proposed more than a decade ago) would build on those memories. A Sportsplex/retail/theater complex might well put them to rest.

Source: The *New York Times*

Check Your Comprehension

1. What is Coney Island?

2. Why is Coney Island important to New York City, according to the author?

3. What are sideshows? Do they still exist?

4. What does this quotation mean: ". . . the value of a place is defined not by dollars and cents but by the quantifiable human energy that was put into it. That energy is more than just construction materials and labor"?

 **READING**

Find out more about **understanding arguments** by looking in the Reference Guide to Reading Strategies on pages xii–xiv.

Understanding Arguments

The author constructs an argument for saving Coney Island, but does so very subtly. What reasons does he give? Below is an outline of a typical structure for an argument. Fill in the information from your understanding of the reading.

Main argument: *Coney Island should be preserved.*

Reason 1.

Reason 2.

Reason 3.

Do you find his argument convincing? Are there any other points you think the author should make?

VOCABULARY
Latin-based Words

Understanding basic Latin word parts can help you to understand new or unfamiliar words. The words below are Latin in their origins. Look at the part of the word that is in **bold** letters. List as many other words as you can with that word part. (Look up any of the words below that you don't understand.)

re**coll**ection   **gen**eration

con**fluen**ce   **quant**ifiable

pre**serv**ationist   con**struct**ion

Word part	Other words
coll	**coll**ege,
fluen	
serv	
gen	
quant	
struct	

THINK ABOUT IT

1. Do you think Coney Island is an important part of New York City's history? Why or why not?

2. Developers often want to replace older buildings or areas with newer ones. Why do you think this happens? Should we work to preserve older places, or should we promote progress?

3. Is there a historic building or place in your community that is important to you? What if it were going to be replaced by a modern shopping mall? Write a letter to the developers of the shopping mall explaining why this place is important to your community.

SYNTHESIS

Discussion and Debate
1. What are the differences between a city and a town? List as many as you can think of.

2. Some of the readings in this chapter have presented generalizations or stereotypes of people in different areas of the United States. Think about the region that you and your family are from. Has it been stereotyped by outside observers? What is the stereotype? Is it accurate? Why or why not?

3. The graph on page 105 shows that the population of the United States is increasingly urban. What do you think of this trend? What are the consequences?

4. Think of another question to ask your classmates about the ideas presented in this chapter.

Writing Topics
1. Read the following topic sentences. Write two sentences supporting each of them.

   a. City life is exciting and interesting.

   1. _____

   2. _____

   b. Country life is slow and boring.

   1. _____

   2. _____

   c. City life is hectic and dangerous.

   1. _____

   2. _____

   d. Country life is peaceful and friendly.

   1. _____

   2. _____

2. Write a letter to a friend in another country. Describe the place where you are living. Include both the negative and positive aspects of it.

3. Would you rather live in the city or the country? Write a short essay and explain your choice.

4. Write in your journal about someplace you would like to live. It can be anywhere in the world. Talk about why this place is appealing to you.

On Your Own

1. Choose a city in the United States that you would be interested in visiting. Write to the Chamber of Commerce of that city, requesting tourist information.

2. Interview two Americans from different parts of the United States. Ask them what it was like growing up where they did. (Or, ask one who grew up in a city and one who grew up in the country.) Take notes or tape record your interviews. Tell your class about your interviews.

3. The following films portray regions of the United States, conflicts between regions, or between city life and country life. Check one out from a library or a video store.
   Town/country conflict: *Crocodile Dundee, The Out-of-Towners, Continental Divide*
   Regional conflict: *Annie Hall* (East versus West), *Mississippi Burning* (North versus South)
   Regional portrayal: *Giant, The Last Picture Show* (Texas), *Cross Creek* (Northern Florida), *Fast Times at Ridgemont High* (California), *Wall Street* (New York)

★★

A L M A N A C   For additional cultural information, refer to the Almanac on pages 221–234. The Almanac contains lists of useful facts, maps, and other information to enhance your learning.

CHAPTER 6

Language

The United States is an English-speaking country, but its linguistic history is complicated. This chapter looks at changes in modern English, and some controversies about the use of languages other than English in the United States.

PART ONE

TRENDS: WAYS WITH WORDS

American English is constantly changing. New products and technology mean new words. This phenomenon is examined here.

Before You Read

The following reading talks about phrases that have special significance in American culture. It contains many phrases that may be unfamiliar to you. As you read, try to imagine the situations to which the author might be referring. For example, the first saying, "Charge!" refers to a battle cry, common in war movies.

Before you read, think about the following questions:

- Are there well known phrases ("lines") from books or movies that are memorable for you, either in English or in your first language?
- Have you ever imagined yourself winning a big prize? What would you say to the audience in your acceptance speech?

The Ten Earliest Words

Word	Date	Word	Date
town	601–604	ward	680
priest	601–604	thing	685–686
earl	616	theft	688–695
this	670	worth	695
streale	680	then	695–696

Source: Oxford English Dictionary, Oxford University Press, Oxford

Cultural Cues

The Academy The Academy of Motion Picture Arts and Sciences; the Academy is responsibly for awarding the Oscars™ every March.

jury duty The responsibility a U.S. citizen has to serve as a member of a jury at a trial.

umpteenth A somewhat large, but vague number; patterned on the other "teen" numbers, such as sixteenth, seventeenth, etc.

About the Author

Christopher Buckley is a humor writer, who is the author of *Thank You for Smoking* and *Wry Martinis*. He is also the son of the prominent conservative writer/commentator, William F. Buckley, Jr.

I Always Wanted to Say That

by Christopher Buckley

For most of us, life is less dramatic than the movies. Few of us will get to deliver the really cool lines, like "Charge!" or "Sponge, clamp, sutures," or "I'd like to thank the Academy." I suppose that most people at some point have imagined themselves saying, "Take her down to periscope depth." Or
5 even, "Fire torpedo tube number one!"

When I was on jury duty recently, I got to say something I never thought possible. The judge was asking us about our suitability to serve. Not wanting to share the particulars of one of my answers, I meekly stuck my hand in the air and asked, "Your Honor, may I approach the bench?"

10 "Approach," he said. I approached, feeling puffed up and important.

The next day I recounted my thrill to my friend Geoff, who happened to have served with the Special Forces in Vietnam. He shared my excitement: "It's like the first time I got to say, 'Cover me.' " This put my big rhetorical moment in perspective.

15 Along the years, however, I did get to utter a few other big lines. I've said, on my knees, "Will you marry me?" A few years later, I said until I was hoarse, "It's a girl!" I've said, from the top of a ship's mast after crossing the ocean, "Land ho!" melodramatic, I admit, but it sounded better than, "Yo, Spain!"

20 A friend of mine tells a story about a magistrate in Scotland. When the town drunk was hauled in before him for the umpteenth time, the magistrate looked down at him and said, "It is the sentence of the court that you be taken from here to the place of execution and there hanged by the neck until you are dead."

25 The drunk fainted. As they were reviving him, the bailiff looked up quizzically at the judge. The judge shrugged and said, "I've just always wanted to say that."

I know exactly how he felt.

Source: *Wry Martinis*

Check Your Comprehension

1. Why did the author feel important after saying "May I approach the bench?"

2. Was the magistrate's judgment serious? How do you know this?

3. What is the main point of this reading?

READING

Find out more about **making inferences** by looking in the Reference Guide to Reading Strategies on pages xii–xiv.

Making Inferences

Buckley doesn't state directly the situations to which he refers in this reading. However, by looking closely at the vocabulary he uses, you can infer what situations he is referring to. Look at the phrases below, taken from the reading, and state in what kind of situation this phrase would be spoken, and whom it would be spoken by. The first one is done for you.

Phrase	Situation	Person
"Sponge, clamp, sutures."	hospital operating room	surgeon
"I'd like to thank the Academy."		
"Take her down to periscope depth. Fire torpedo tube number one!"		
"Land ho!"		
"Your honor, may I approach the bench?"		
"Cover me!"		

VOCABULARY
Professional Terms

One of the advantages of professional terminology is that it provides a short way to refer to a more complicated idea or object. Here are some professional terms found in the article. What is their "plain English" meaning? You may need to describe them in a sentence.

1. *periscope depth* _____

_____

2. *sutures* _____

_____

3. *the bench* _____

_____

4. *bailiff* _____

_____

5. *magistrate* _____

_____

THINK ABOUT IT

1. Are there things you've "always wanted to say"? What are they?

2. Do you know the professional terminology of a certain job? What is it? Make a list of terms that might be unfamiliar to someone who doesn't know about this job.

3. Interview someone whose job is unfamiliar to you. Ask her or him about the terminology of his or her job. Create a small glossary of words that are particular to that job.

Before You Read

Soft Drink Consumption in the United States

	Brand	Sales in 1994 (gallons)
1	Coca-Cola	2,621,000,000
2	Pepsi	2,066,000,000
3	Diet Coke	1,268,000,000
4	Dr. Pepper	768,000,000
5	Diet Pepsi	760,000,000
6	Mountain Dew	683,000,000
7	Sprite	581,000,000
8	7-Up	381,000,000
9	Caffeine-Free Diet Coke	265,000,000
10	Caffeine-Free Diet Pepsi	153,000,000
	TOTAL	13,275,000,000
	Amount per person	50 gallons

Source: *The Top 10 of Everything, 1996*, Dorling Kindersley, New York: 1995

In this article, the writer discusses a particularly American phenomenon: the unusually large size of products in America. Most people traveling to the United States note how large, for example, soft drinks are. Conversely, most Americans traveling abroad find drink containers very small.

Before you read, think about the following questions:

- Have you ever ordered a "large" drink in a movie theater? How big was it?

- How large is a "large" drink in your home country? Is it similar or different from a "large" in the United States?

Cultural Cues

flagon of mead Mead is a very old drink, popular in the Middle Ages. A *flagon* is a cup.

7-Eleven A chain of small convenience stores, open late hours.

7-Eleven Big Gulp

☕ Make Mine a Medium

by Cynthia Crossen

Try ordering a medium coffee at most coffee bars. They look at you as though you asked for a flagon of mead.

The word medium, especially in food and beverages, is going the way of the "cup" of coffee. Drink sizes have become a free-for-all of image
5 building, divorced from any real description of quantity.

The move away from medium is partly attributable to economics—companies trying to squeeze out a few more cents by exaggerating sizes.

To be sure, medium hasn't died altogether. There are medium olives (along with large, giant, jumbo and colossal) and medium garbage bags.
10 There are medium eggs: they are often the smallest. Bigger eggs are classified as large, extra-large and jumbo. Paper towels now come in large and jumbo too.

Small products are flourishing, but they aren't called small. For example, cereals, aspirin and shampoo are sold in tiny packages. "But they're never
15   called tiny," says Lorna Opatow, president of the marketing research firm of Opatow Associates. "They're called individual or one-time or disposable."

When it comes to sizing, the masters are fast-food restaurants. At McDonald's the soft-drink sizes are regular, medium, large and, on occasion, super-size. "Nobody wants a small drink anymore," says McDonald's spokesman
20   Chuck Ebeling. "We live in an era when people carry a liter bottle of water as though it were a pencil over their ear."

At Burger King there are still small, medium and large drinks. But what do those words mean? In 1954, when the chain started, it called a 12-ounce regular and a 16-ounce large. Today the small is 16 ounces and the large is
25   32 ounces.

The king of more is 7-Eleven, which boasts that it makes America's biggest drink, the 64-ounce Double Gulp. Karen Raskopf, a 7-Eleven spokeswoman, says no other country gulps as America does: the chain's international stores don't sell the Double Gulp. Indeed in Europe and Japan a small
30   size is often equated with luxury—the 6½-ounce Perrier bottle, for example.

Behind the size inflation in beverages is a simple fact: the actual cost of the additional beverage is a minute portion of the price. "The packaging and handling costs for a drink are a substantial part of the cost," says Ebeling of McDonald's. "If we package it in a larger size, that's more efficient for us."
35   Amazingly, Pasqua Coffee, a national chain based in San Francisco, is sticking with small, medium and large. "We want to offer quick service," says Robert Mann, vice president of operations. "We don't want to waste time correcting customers' coffee grammar."

Source: *Wall Street Journal*

Check Your Comprehension

1. What are the reasons for "size inflation" in the United States?

2. Why aren't enormous drink sizes popular in Europe or Japan?

3. What kinds of small-sized products are selling well?

4. What is the author's point of view on this trend toward larger sizes?

5. Why does Pasqua Coffee still offer "small, medium, and large" sizes?

READING

Find out more about **summarizing** by looking in the Reference Guide to Reading Strategies on pages xii–xiv.

Summarizing

What are the main ideas in this article? Summarize the article in the following box. Compare your summary with a classmate's. What details did you include and which ones did you leave out? Would you rewrite your summary after reading your partner's?

_____

_____

_____

_____

_____

_____

_____

_____

_____

_____

_____

_____

VOCABULARY
Colloquial Phrases

This article contains several colloquial phrases that may be difficult to understand or to look up in a standard dictionary. Complete the following sentences, showing that you understand the meaning of the phrase taken from the reading.

1. If you try to _____, they **look at you as if** you were

   _____ .

2. The _____ became a **free-for-all** after _____ .

3. I tried to **squeeze out** _____ .

4. _____ **come in** either medium or large.

5. When it **comes to** _____, I am an expert.

THINK ABOUT IT

1. Americans are often said to like big things: big houses, big cars, and now big cups of coffee. Do you think this is a fair characterization? Why might it be the case? Can you think of any exceptions to this?

2. What are some of the drawbacks of enjoying large-sized products?

3. Visit a supermarket in your neighborhood. Note the sizes of the following items:

Product	Smallest size	Largest size
Breakfast cereal		
Potato chips		
Milk		
Cookies		
Laundry detergent		
Soft drinks		
Canned vegetables		
Packages of rice		

Are there any products that have a larger size range than others? Why might this be so?

PART TWO

CONTROVERSY: FIGHTING WORDS

Should everyone in the United States learn to speak English? Should children be taught in languages other than English? These are controversial questions in the United States. Public opinion varies, and governments try to enact laws that deal with these questions. However, it is clear that these will be controversial subjects in the future, as they have been in the past.

Before You Read

English as an official language, State laws

State	Notes
Alabama	Official language
Arizona	English as the language
Arkansas	Official language
California	Official language
Colorado	Official language
Florida	English is the official language of Florida
Georgia	English designated as official language
Guam	Official languages
Hawaii	Official languages
Illinois	Official language of state
Kentucky	State language
Louisiana	Publication of advertisements notices etc. in English language. But duplication in French permitted
Mississippi	State language
Montana	English as official and primary language of state and local governments
Nebraska	English language to be official
North Carolina	Official language
North Dakota	Official language
Tennessee	English—official and legal language
Virginia	English designated the official language of the Commonwealth
Wyoming	Official language

In this reading, the author tells his own story of learning English as a child. As you read, think about the following questions:

- Do other members of your family speak English? How has that affected your English education?
- Is language use different within a family than it is in public? In what ways?

Cultural Cues

gringos Typically white North Americans or English speakers.

Safeway A large chain of grocery stores.

barrio Spanish word for *neighborhood*, usually referring to neighborhoods in which the majority of residents are Spanish-speaking.

About the Author

Richard Rodriguez was born in San Francisco, CA and raised in Sacramento, California. He earned his B.A. at Stanford University, a masters degree at Columbia University, and did graduate study at the University of California, Berkeley and the Warburg Institute in London. He is known for his autobiography, *Hunger of Memory: The Education of Richard Rodriguez* (1982), from which this reading is taken. His second book, *Days of Obligation*, (1992) was a finalist for the Pulitzer Prize. He writes for major American magazines and appears on "The News Hour with Jim Lehrer" on PBS.

Aria

by Richard Rodriguez

I was a listening child, careful to hear the very different sounds of Spanish and English. Wide-eyed with hearing, I'd listen to sounds more than words. First, there were English 5 (*gringo)* sounds. So many words were still unknown that when the butcher or the lady at the drugstore said something to me, exotic polysyllabic sounds would bloom in the midst of their sentences. Often, the speech of people 10 in public seemed to me very loud, booming with confidence. The man behind the counter would literally ask, "What can I do for you?" But by being so firm and so clear, the sound of his voice said that he was a *gringo*; he be-15 longed in public society.

I would also hear then the high nasal notes of middle-class American speech. The air stirred with sound. Sometimes, even now, when I have been traveling abroad for several 20 weeks, I will hear what I heard as a boy. In hotel lobbies or airports, in Turkey or Brazil, some Americans will pass, and suddenly I will hear it again—the high sound of American voices. For a few 25 seconds I will hear it with pleasure, for it is now the sound of *my* society—a reminder of home. But inevitably—already on the flight headed for home—the sound fades with repeti-30 tion. I will be unable to hear it anymore.

When I was a boy, things were different. The accent of *los gringos* was never pleasing nor was it hard 35 to hear. Crowds at Safeway or at bus stops would be noisy with sound. And I would be forced to edge away form the chirping chatter above me.

I was unable to hear my own sounds, but 40 I knew very well that I spoke English poorly. My words could not stretch far enough to form complete thoughts. And the words I did speak I didn't know well enough to make into distinct sounds. (Listeners would usually lower their 45 heads, better to hear what I was trying to say.) But it was one thing for *me* to speak English with difficulty. It was more troubling for me to hear my parents speak in public: their high-whining vowels and guttural consonants; their 50 sentences that got stuck with 'ch' and 'ah' sounds; the confused syntax; the hesitant rhythm of sounds so different from the way *gringos* spoke. I'd notice, moreover, that my parents' voices were softer than those of 55 *gringos* we'd meet.

I am tempted now to say that none of this mattered. In adulthood I am embarrassed by childhood fears. And, in a way, it didn't matter very much that my parents could not speak

60 English with ease. Their linguistic difficulties had no serious consequences. My mother and father made themselves understood at the county hospital clinic and at government of-fices. And yet, in another way, it mattered very
65 much—it was unsettling to hear my parents struggle with English. Hearing them, I'd grow nervous, my clutching trust in their protection and power weakened.

There were many times like the night at
70 a brightly lit gasoline station (a blaring white memory) when I stood uneasily, hearing my father. He was talking to a teenaged attendant. I do not recall what they were saying, but I cannot forget the sounds my father made as
75 he spoke. At one point his words slid together to form one word—sounds as confused as the threads of blue and green oil in the puddle next to my shoes. His voice rushed through what he had left to say. And, toward the end, reached
80 falsetto notes, appealing to his listener's under-standing. I looked away to the lights of passing automobiles. I tried not to hear anymore. But I heard only too well the calm, easy tones in the attendant's reply. Shortly afterward, walking
85 toward home with my father, I shivered when he put his hand on my shoulder. The first chance that I got, I evaded his grasp and ran on ahead into the dark, skipping with feigned boyish exuberance.

90 But then there was Spanish. *Español:* my family's language. *Español:* the language that seemed to me a private language. I'd hear strangers on the radio and in the Mexican Cath-olic church across town speaking in Spanish,
95 but I couldn't really believe that Spanish was a public language, like English. Spanish speak-ers, rather, seemed related to me, for I sensed that we shared—through our language—the experience of feeling apart from *los gringos.*
100 It was thus a ghetto Spanish that I heard and I spoke. Like those whose lives are bound by a barrio, I was reminded by Spanish of my separateness from *los otros, los gringos* in power. But more intensely than for most barrio
105 children—because I did not live in a barrio—Spanish seemed to me the language of home.

(Most days it was only at home that I'd hear it.) It became the language of joyful return.

A family member would say something to
110 me and I would feel myself specially recog-nized. My parents would say something to me and I would feel embraced by the sounds of their words. Those sounds said: *I am speaking with ease in Spanish. I am addressing you in*
115 *words I never use with* los gringos. *I recognize you as someone special, close, like no one out-side. You belong with us. In the family.*
(Ricardo.)

At the age of five, six, well past the time
120 when most other children no longer easily no-tice the difference between sounds uttered at home and words spoken in public, I had a dif-ferent experience. I lived in a world magically compounded of sounds. I remained a child
125 longer than most; I lingered too long, poised at the edge of language—often frightened by the sounds of *los gringos,* delighted by the sounds of Spanish at home. I shared with my family a language that was startlingly different
130 from that used in the great city around us.

For me there were none of the gradations between public and private society so normal to a maturing child. Outside the house was public society; inside the house was private.
135 Just opening or closing the screen door behind me was an important experience. I'd rarely leave home all alone or without reluctance. Walking down the sidewalk, under the canopy of tall trees, I'd warily notice the—suddenly—
140 silent neighborhood kids who stood warily watching me. Nervously, I'd arrive at the gro-cery store to hear there the sounds of the *gringo*—foreign to me—reminding me that in this world so big, I was a foreigner. But then
145 I'd return. Walking back toward our house, climbing the steps from the sidewalk, when the front door was open in summer, I'd hear voices beyond the screen door talking in Spanish. For a second or two, I'd stay, linger there, listening.
150 Smiling, I'd hear my mother call out, saying in Spanish (words): "Is that you, Richard?" All the while her sounds would assure me: *You are home now; come closer; inside. With us.*

"*Sí*," I'd reply.

155 Once more inside the house I would resume (assume) my place in the family. The sounds would dim, grow harder to hear. Once more at home, I would grow less aware of that fact. It required, however, no more than the blurt of 160 the doorbell to alert me to listen to sounds all over again. The house would turn instantly still while my mother went to the door. I'd hear her hard English sounds. I'd wait to hear her voice return to soft-sounding Spanish, which assured 165 me, as surely as did the clicking tongue of the lock on the door, that the stranger was gone.

Source: *Hunger of Memory: The Education of Richard Rodriguez*

Check Your Comprehension

1. What characteristics does the author associate with public language?

2. What characteristics does the author associate with private language?

3. How did the author feel about his parents' English abilities?

4. What does the author mean when he says "it didn't matter very much that my parents could not speak English with ease"?

5. What is the author's main point?

READING

Find out more about **understanding contrasts** by looking in the Reference Guide to Reading Strategies on pages xii–xiv.

Understanding Contrasts

In this essay, Rodriguez draws contrasts between his private Spanish-speaking world and the public English-speaking one. Review the reading, and list the points on which he contrasts the two worlds. The first one is done for you.

English-speaking world	Spanish-speaking world
1. public	private
2.	
3.	
4.	
5.	

Review these contrasts. What conclusion do you think Rodriguez draws based on these ideas?

VOCABULARY
Paraphrasing

The following phrases are taken from the reading. Paraphrase them, that is, put them in your own words. Refer to the reading to see the context of these phrases.

1. exotic polysyllabic sounds would bloom in the midst of their sentences

_____

_____

2. I would be forced to edge away from the chirping chatter.

_____

_____

3. their high-whining vowels and guttural consonants

_____

_____

4. my clutching trust in their protection and power weakened

_____

_____

5. and toward the end, reached falsetto notes, appealing to his listener's understanding

_____

_____

6. there were none of the gradations between public and private society

_____

_____

THINK ABOUT IT

1. Are any of your experiences learning English similar to Rodriguez's? Why or why not?

2. How is "family" or "private" language important to Rodriguez? Is it important to you?

3. Interview a classmate about his or her experience learning to speak English. Write a short report in which you compare and contrast your partner's experience with your own.

Before You Read

Language Spoken at Home and Ability to Speak English

Rank	Language	Total	English Ability			
			Very Well	Well	Not Well	Not at All
	United States	230,445,777				
	English Only	198,600,798				
	Total Non-English	31,844,979	17,862,477	7,310,301	4,826,958	845,243
1	Spanish	17,339,172	9,033,407	3,804,792	3,040,828	460,145
2	French	1,702,176	1,226,043	318,409	149,505	8,219
3	German	1,547,099	1,161,127	284,809	96,804	4,359
4	Italian	1,308,648	874,032	283,354	134,114	17,148
5	Chinese	1,249,213	496,277	379,720	264,240	108,976
6	Tagalog	843,251	556,252	223,971	58,320	4,708
7	Polish	723,483	455,551	169,548	85,298	13,086
8	Korean	626,478	242,939	195,120	154,617	33,802
9	Vietnamese	507,069	186,207	177,689	118,180	24,993
10	Portuguese	429,860	235,283	96,243	71,305	27,029

Source: U.S. Bureau of the Census, 1990 Census of Population

In the following essay, the author looks at the effectiveness of bilingual education, the practice of teaching children in two languages, English and their native tongue.

Before you read, think about the following questions:

- What do you know about bilingual education? Is it popular in your home country?

- Do you think immigrants should be required to learn English? Why or why not?

Cultural Cues

E Pluribus Unum The motto of the United States, Latin for "from many comes one."

PTA meeting PTA stands for "Parent-Teacher Association." The PTA is a part of most American public schools and provides support for schools and families.

"Rockwellesque" Referring to the American artist, Norman Rockwell; "Rockwellesque" means similar in character to Rockwell's work. Rockwell was known for paintings that portrayed idealized views of American life. His work is still greatly beloved, though considered sentimental.

About the Author   James Fallows is the Washington editor of *The Atlantic Monthly* magazine. He studied at Harvard and at Oxford. He spent many years in Asia and wrote extensively about Japan. He is the author of *More Like Us: Making America Great Again.*

BILINGUAL EDUCATION

by James Fallows

A national culture is held together by official rules and informal signals. Through their language, dress, taste, and habits of life, immigrants initially violate the rules and confuse
5 the signals. The United States has prided itself on building a nation out of diverse parts. *E Pluribus Unum* originally referred to the act of political union in which separate colonies became one sovereign state. It now seems
10 more fitting as a token of the cultural adjustments through which immigrant strangers have become Americans. Can the assimilative forces still prevail?

The question arises because most of today's
15 immigrants share one trait: their native language is Spanish.

From 1970 to 1978, the three leading sources of legal immigrants to the U.S. were Mexico, the Philippines, and Cuba. About 42
20 percent of legal immigration during the seventies was from Latin America. It is thought that about half of all illegal immigrants come from Mexico, and 10 to 15 percent more from elsewhere in Latin America. Including illegal immi-
25 grants makes all figures imprecise, but it seems reasonable to conclude that more than half the people who now come to the United States

speak Spanish. This is a greater concentration of immigrants in one non-English language
30 group than ever before.

Is it a threat? The conventional wisdom about immigrants and their languages is that the Spanish-speakers are asking for treatment different from that which has been accorded
35 to everybody else. In the old days, it is said, immigrants were eager to assimilate as quickly as possible. They were placed, sink or swim, in English-language classrooms, and they swam. But now the Latin Americans seem to be in-
40 sisting on bilingual classrooms and ballots. "The Hispanics demand that the United States become a bilingual country, with all children entitled to be taught in the language of their heritage, at public expense," Theodore White
45 has written. Down this road lie the linguistic cleavages that have brought grief to other nations.

This is the way many people think, and this is the way I myself thought as I began this
50 project.

The historical parallel closest to today's concentration of Spanish-speaking immigrants is the German immigration of the nineteenth century. From 1830 to 1890, 4.5 million

55 Germans emigrated to the United States, making up one third of the immigrant total. The Germans recognized that command of English would finally ensure for them, and especially for their children, a place in the mainstream 60 of American society. But like the Swedes, Dutch, and French before them, they tried hard to retain the language in which they had been raised.

The midwestern states, where Germans 65 were concentrated, established bilingual schools, in which children could receive instruction in German. In Ohio, German-English public schools were in operation by 1840; in 1837, the Pennsylvania legislature ordered that 70 German-language public schools be established on an equal basis with English-language schools. Minnesota, Maryland, and Indiana also operated public schools in which German was used, either by itself or in addition to English.

75 In *Life with Two Languages*, his study of bilingualism, François Grosjean says, "What is particularly striking about German Americans in the nine- 80 teenth century is their constant efforts to maintain their language, culture, and heritage."

75 Yet despite everything the Germans could do, their lan- 85 guage began to die out. The progression was slow and fraught with pain. For the immigrant, language was the main source of certainty and connec- 90 tion to the past. As the children broke from the Old World culture and tried out their snappy English slang on their parents, the pride the parents felt at 95 such achievements was no doubt mixed with the bitter-sweet awareness that they were losing control.

At first the children would 100 act as interpreters for their par-

ents; then they would demand the independence appropriate to that role; then they would yearn to escape the coarse ways of immigrant life. And in the end, they would be Americans. 105 It was hard on the families, but it built an assimilated English-language culture.

The pattern of assimilation is familiar from countless novels, as well as from the experience of many people now living. Why, then, is 110 the currently fashionable history of assimilation so different? Why is it assumed, in so many discussions of bilingual education, that in the old days immigrants switched quickly and enthusiastically to English?

115 One reason is that the experience of Jewish immigrants in the early twentieth century was different from this pattern. German Jews, successful and thoroughly assimilated here in the nineteenth century, oversaw an effort to bring 120 Eastern European Jews into the American

mainstream as quickly as possible. In New York City, the Lower East Side's Hebrew Institute, later known as the Educational Alliance, defined its goal as teaching the newcomers "the
125 privileges and duties of American citizenship." Although many Jewish immigrants preserved their Yiddish, Jews generally learned English faster than any other group.

Another reason that nineteenth-century lin-
130 guistic history is so little remembered lies in the political experience of the early twentieth century. As an endless stream of New Immigrants arrived from Eastern Europe, the United States was awash in theories about the threats
135 the newcomers posed to American economic, sanitary, and racial standards, and the "100 percent Americanism" movement arose. By the late 1880s, school districts in the Midwest had already begun reversing their early encourage-
140 ment of bilingual education. Competence in English was made a requirement for naturalized citizens in 1906. Pro-English-language leagues sprang up to help initiate the New Immigrants. California's Commission on Immigra-
145 tion and Housing, for example, endorsed a campaign of "Americanization propaganda" in light of "the necessity for all to learn English— the language of America." With the coming of World War I, all German-language activities
150 were suddenly cast in a different light. Eventually as a result, Americans came to believe that previous immigrants had speedily switched to English, and to view the Hispanics' attachment to Spanish as a troubling aberration.
155 The bilingual system is accused of supporting a cadre of educational consultants while actually retarding the students' progress into the English-speaking mainstream. In this view, bilingual education could even be laying the
160 foundation for a separate Hispanic culture, by extending the students' Spanish-language world from their homes to their schools.

Before I traveled to some of the schools in which bilingual education was applied, I shared
165 the skeptics' view. What good could come of a system that encouraged, to whatever degree, a language other than the national tongue? But after visiting elementary, junior high, and high schools in Miami, Houston, San Antonio, Aus-
170 tin, several parts of Los Angeles, and San Diego, I found little connection between the political debate over bilingual education and what was going on in these schools.

To begin with, one central fact about bilin-
175 gual education goes largely unreported. It is a *temporary* program. The time a typical student stays in the program varies from place to place—often two years in Miami, three years in Los Angeles—but when that time has passed,
180 the student will normally leave. Why, then, do bilingual programs run through high school? Those classes are usually for students who are new to the district—usually because their parents are new to the country.
185 There is another fact about bilingual education, more difficult to prove but impressive to me, a hostile observer. Most of the children I saw were unmistakably learning to speak English.
190 In the elementary schools, where the children have come straight out of all-Spanish environments, the background babble seems to be entirely in Spanish. The kindergarten and first-to third-grade classrooms I saw were festooned
195 with the usual squares and circles cut from colored construction paper, plus posters featuring Big Bird and charts about the weather and the seasons. Most of the schools seemed to keep a rough balance between English and
200 Spanish in the lettering around the room; the most Spanish environment I saw was in one school in East Los Angeles, where about a third of the signs were in English.

The elementary school teachers were
205 mostly Mexican-American women. They prompted the children with a mixture of English and Spanish during the day. While books in both languages are available in the classrooms, most of the first-grade reading drills I
210 saw were in Spanish. In theory, children will learn the phonetic principle of reading more quickly if they are not trying to learn a new

language at the same time. Once comfortable as readers, they will theoretically be able to transfer their ability to English.

In a junior high school in Houston, I saw a number of Mexican and Salvadoran students in their "bilingual" biology and math classes. They were drilled entirely in Spanish on the parts of an amoeba and on the difference between a parallelogram and a rhombus. When students enter bilingual programs at this level, the goal is to keep them current with the standard curriculum while introducing them to English. I found my fears of linguistic separatism rekindled by the sight of fourteen-year-olds lectured to in Spanish. I reminded myself that many of the students I was seeing had six months earlier lived in another country.

The usual next stop for students whose time in bilingual education is up is a class in intensive English, lasting one to three hours a day. These students are divided into two or three proficiency levels, from those who speak no English to those nearly ready to forgo special help. In Houston, a teacher drilled two-dozen high-school-age Cambodians, Indians, Cubans, and Mexicans on the crucial difference between the voiced *th* sound of "this" and the voiceless *th* of "thing." In Miami, a class of high school sophomores included youths from Cuba, El Salvador, and Honduras. They listened as their teacher read a Rockwellesque essay about a student with a crush on his teacher, and then set to work writing an essay of their own, working in words like "garrulous" and "sentimentalize."

One of the students in Miami, a sixteen-year-old from Honduras, said that his twelve-year-old brother had already moved into mainstream classes. Linguists say this is the standard pattern for immigrant children. The oldest children hold on to their first language longest, while their younger sisters and brothers swim quickly into the new language culture.

The more I saw of the classes, the more convinced I became that most of the students were learning English. Therefore, I started to wonder what it is about bilingual education that has made it the focus of such bitter disagreement.

For one thing, most immigrant groups other than Hispanics take a comparatively dim view of bilingual education. Haitians, Vietnamese, and Cambodians are eligible for bilingual education, but in general they are unenthusiastic. In Miami, Haitian boys and girls may learn to read in Creole rather than English. Still, their parents push to keep them moving into English. "A large number of [Haitian] parents come to the PTA meetings, and they don't want interpreters," said the principal of Miami's Edison Park Elementary School last spring. They want to learn English. They don't want notices coming home in three languages. When they come here, unless there is total non-communication, they will try to get through to us in their broken English. The students learn the language *very* quickly."

Source: *Atlantic Monthly*

Check Your Comprehension

1. What is the argument against bilingual education, as presented in this article?

2. Why did the German language "die out" in the United States?

3. Why did the author change his mind about bilingual education?

📖 READING

Find out more about **understanding processes** by looking in the Reference Guide to Reading Strategies on pages xii–xiv.

Understanding Processes

Review the process by which the German language died out among German immigrants to the United States. Summarize that process in chronological order: that is, what happened first, second, third, etc.? The first step is done for you.

Step 1. From 1830-1890, 4.5 million Germans emigrated to the United States.

_____

Step 2. _____

_____

_____

Step 3. _____

_____

_____

Step 4. _____

_____

_____

Step 5. _____

_____

_____

Step 6. _____

_____

_____

Add more steps if you need to. Compare your answers with those of a partner.

VOCABULARY
The Language of Politics

Look up the following words in your dictionary. Read the definitions carefully, then rewrite the definitions in your own words. Write an example sentence for each word that shows you know what it means. You may want to work with a partner.

1. *assimilation* _____

_____

Example sentence: _____

2. *ballot* _____

_____

Example sentence: _____

3. *cadre* _____

_____

Example sentence: _____

4. *ideologue* _____

_____

Example sentence: _____

5. *mobility* _____

_____

Example sentence: _____

6. *naturalization* _____

_____

Example sentence: _____

7. *separatism* _____

_____

Example sentence: _____

8. *sovereign* _____

_____

Example sentence: _____

THINK ABOUT IT

 Watch the CNN video on bilingual education.

Discuss these questions:

1. What are the benefits of bilingual education?

2. Why are some people against bilingual education?

3. What did you learn from this video clip?

1. Bilingual education is a very controversial topic. Based on the reading and your own understanding of it, what is the controversy about? With which side do you agree?

2. Look in a newspaper or on the Internet for articles about "English Only" laws. What do these laws do? Are you in favor of such laws?

3. Does making laws about language make sense to you? Why or why not?

SYNTHESIS

Discussion and Debate

1. What has been the effect of English on your first language? Discuss this both from a personal perspective and a national perspective.

2. What is the role of slang in language? Do you know American slang? Do you use it? Why or why not?

3. Organize a debate in your class on one of the following topics:

   • English Only laws

   • Bilingual Education

   • Foreign language requirements at universities

   To challenge your debating skills, take the side you *don't* agree with and argue effectively for that opinion.

Writing Topics

1. Choose an idiom or word in English whose history interests you. Consult an idiom dictionary or a dictionary that gives histories of words. Write a short report (one or two paragraphs) on the history and meaning of the word or phrase you chose.

2. Write a one-page essay describing the use of English in your home country. Is it required in school? Is it used in business? What else might be interesting about it?

3. Write an argument essay (two or more pages) about a linguistic issue that is important to you. Discuss your choice of topic with your

teacher before beginning. In your essay, you should include the following:

- Background for the issue: What are the important facts that a reader should know about your topic?
- Your argument: What do you want the reader to believe after reading your paper?
- Your consideration of the other side: Are there some opposing viewpoints that might make some sense? Describe those briefly, and explain why they are less compelling than your view.

4. Write about your experience learning English. Be sure to include examples from your experience, not just opinions. Review Rodriguez's writing as an example.

On Your Own

1. Talk to a native English speaker about his or her opinions of current English. You might ask these questions (be sure to add your own, too):

- Do you think English is changing? How?
- Do you think the changes are good?
- Are there any trends in modern English you don't like?
- What's your favorite slang word? Least favorite?
- Do you think it's okay to use profanity (to swear)?

Summarize your discussion and report your findings to your class.

2. Watch a video or film that deals with the subject of bilingualism or language learning. Some you might consider are: *The Miracle Worker*, *Children of a Lesser God*, *The Joy Luck Club*, *Iron and Silk*, or *Moscow on the Hudson*. Write a review of the film you watched. Would you recommend it to others? Why or why not?

3. Try to be aware of new words—slang, new professional terms, etc.—for one or two days. Write anything you don't understand in your journal. Then, ask others for help in understanding those words. Compile a report of your experience.

★★

A L M A N A C For additional cultural information, refer to the Almanac on pages 221–234. The Almanac contains lists of useful facts, maps, and other information to enhance your learning.

★★★

Virtues and Vices

America is known as a land of generosity and good deeds. Unfortunately, it also is a land where such vices as alcohol consumption, cigarette smoking, and drug taking are popular. This chapter looks at some of the virtues and vices that affect Americans.

Virtues: A Friend in Need

How do you feel about your neighbors?
Are they your friends, or just people who happen to live nearby?
This section looks at different aspects of being a neighbor.

Source: *World Factbook*

Before You Read

Population Density of Selected Countries

Country	Persons/ square kilometer	Country	Persons/ square kilometer
Russia	8.67	Philippines	253.68
United States	27.83	Israel	266.47
Mexico	49.46	El Salvador	269.10
Greece	80.46	India	294.07
France	107.14	Lebanon	331.69
Indonesia	109.29	Japan	332.77
China	127.29	South Korea	466.58
Dominican Republic	161.48	Taiwan	603.11
Italy	188.66	Singapore	5313.81
Vietnam	227.95		

In the following passage by Andy Rooney, the author discusses the relationships Americans have with their neighbors. He also talks about the "typical" American neighborhood.

Before you read, think about the following questions:

- Are neighbors usually friends in your culture?
- What type of relationship do you have with your neighbors?

About the Author

Andy Rooney began his writing career as a correspondent for *The Stars and Stripes*, a military newspaper, during World War II. Since then he has written for television and many newspapers. He is currently well known for his short, humorous weekly contribution to the television news program *60 Minutes*, which is broadcast on CBS on Sunday nights.

by Andy Rooney Love Thy Neighbor

It seems to me that neighbors are going out of style in America. The friend next door from whom you borrowed four eggs or a ladder has moved, and the people in there now are strangers.

Some of the old folklore of neighborliness is impractical or silly, and it
5 may be just as well that our relations with our neighbors are changing. The biblical commandment to "Love Thy Neighbor" was probably a poor translation of what must have originally been "Respect Thy Neighbor." Love can't be called up on order.

Fewer than half the people in the United States live in the same house
10 they lived in five years ago, so there's no reason to love the people who live next door to you just because they happened to wander into a real estate office that listed the place next door to yours. The only thing neighbors have in common to begin with is proximity, and unless something more develops, that isn't reason enough to be best friends. It sometimes happens
15 naturally, but the chances are very small that your neighbors will be your choice as buddies. Or that you will be theirs, either.

The best relationship with neighbors is one of friendly distance. You say hello, you small-talk if you see them in the yard, you discuss problems as they arise and you help each other in an emergency. It's the kind of arrange-
20 ment where you see more of them in the summer than in the winter. The driveway or the hedge or the fence between you is not really a cold shoulder, but a clear boundary. We all like clearly defined boundaries for ourselves.

If neighbors have changed, neighborhoods have not. They still comprise the same elements. If you live in a real neighborhood you can be sure most
25 of the following people will be found there:

—One family with more kids than they can take care of.

—A dog that gets into garbage cans.

—One grand home with a family so rich that they really aren't part of the neighborhood.

30 —A bad kid who steals or sets fire to things, although no one has ever been able to prove it.

—People who leave their Christmas decorations up until March.

—A grouchy woman who won't let the kids cut through her back-yard.

35 —Someone who doesn't cut their grass more than twice a summer.

—Someone who cuts their grass twice a week and one of the times always seems to be Sunday morning at 7:30.

—One driveway with a junky-looking pickup truck or trailer that's always sitting there.

40 —A family that never seems to turn off any lights in the house.

—A teenager who plays the radio too loud in the summer with the windows open.

—Someone who leaves their barking dog out until 11:30 most nights.

—One mystery couple. They come and go but hardly anyone ever sees them and no one knows what they do.

—A couple that has loud parties all the time with guests that take an hour to leave once they get outside and start shouting good-bye to each other.

—Someone who doesn't pull the shades.

—A house with a big maple tree whose owners don't rake the leaves until most of them have blown into someone else's yard.

It is easier to produce nostalgia about a neighborhood than about a community, but a community is probably a better unit. A neighborhood is just a bunch of individuals who live in proximity, but a community is a group of people who rise above their individual limitations to get some things done in town.

Source: *And More by Andy Rooney*

Check Your Comprehension

1. Why does the author think it is "just as well" that Americans' relationships with neighbors may be changing?

2. What does the author think is the best relationship to have with neighbors?

3. What is the difference between a community and a neighborhood, according to Rooney? Under what circumstances might they be the same?

READING

Find out more about **understanding definitions** by looking in the Reference Guide to Reading Strategies on pages xii–xiv.

Understanding Definitions

How does the author define the following terms? Write your answer in the blanks.

1. *neighbor* _____

_____

2. *neighborhood* _____

_____

3. *community* _____

_____

4. *friendship* _____

_____

5. *love* _____

_____

Next, check your dictionary, and summarize the definitions:

6. *neighbor* _____

_____

7. *neighborhood* _____

_____

8. *community* _____

_____

9. *friendship* _____

_____

10. *love* _____

_____

Compare the two definitions. Discuss any differences or similarities you see with your classmates.

VOCABULARY
Crosswords

Following is a crossword puzzle. Read the definitions, and then write the word that fits each definition in the blanks. All of the words can be found in the reading.

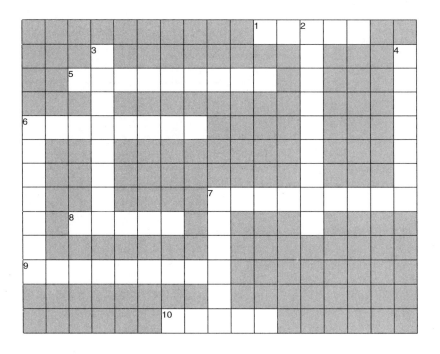

Across

1. A type of wall creating a boundary between two pieces of land

5. A group of people living together who may share interests or beliefs

6. A piece of land found behind a house, usually covered with grass

7. Nearness to; in _____ to

8. A row of bushes or trees that makes up a border or boundary

9. Light conversation about unimportant subjects (hyphenated word)

10. A tree whose leaves turn color and fall in the autumn

Down

2. Fondness for things in the past

3. The knowledge and habits from an earlier time, still in use by a group of people

4. Bad-tempered

6. Friends, pals (informal)

7. A type of small truck

THINK ABOUT IT

1. How are U.S. neighborhood relationships different from those in your culture, in your opinion?

2. What is your neighborhood like? Does it have any of the "characters" that are described in the reading? Are you one of those neighborhood characters?

3. To what community or communities do you belong? For example, you are probably a member of a college or school community.

4. In your journal, write a description of the most important community you belong to. What function does that community serve for you? What benefits do its members get from it? What are the problems with this community?

Before You Read

Charity and a Good Economy, 1995

- The average American household in 1995 contributed about $1,017 to charity—a gain of 10 percent from 1993.

- Americans gave on average 2.2 percent of their income, up from 2.1 percent in 1993.

- Approximately 93 million Americans donated 20 billion hours to charity in 1995—one billion hours more than in 1993.

- Valued at just the minimum wage, time donated amounted to $95 billion.

- Households with a net worth of $25,000 to $50,000 contribute an average of 1.3 percent of their income to charity.

- In the $250,000 to $500,000 range, giving is 2.8 percent of income.

- Those worth $50 million or more give an average of 18 percent of their incomes to charity.

In the following reading, the author describes "Operation Santa Claus," a campaign to donate gifts to poor children.

Before you read, think about the following questions:

- What does charity mean to you?

- Have you ever participated in a volunteer activity? What was the experience like?

Cultural Cues

Manhattan The central borough (area) of New York City.

Penn Station A major transportation center in New York City.

Madison Square Garden A large entertainment arena in New York City; concerts and sporting events are held there.

Queens One of the five boroughs that make up New York City; it is mostly a residential area.

Brooklyn A borough of New York City, known for the Brooklyn Bridge and the Coney Island amusement area.

"Cats" A popular Broadway musical play.

Volunteer Angels

by Verena Dobnik

The envelope is addressed simply to "Dear Santa." The letter inside pleads, politely.

"May you get me a willchair. I need the willchair to be powered. I need it to get around . . . Can you help me Santa? I would do anything for this
5 . . . Love allways, Miracle Retrina."

The 9-year-old, born with no arms and only one functional leg, wrote the faint, crooked words by pushing a pencil with her left foot. Now Miracle Retrina Womack awaits a miracle, and Guillermina "Gigi" Colón is ready to help.

10 "This is what life is really about," Colón says, clutching the child's note as she dashes through the cavernous halls of the General Post Office in

Manhattan, smiling at co-workers who greet her with "Hi Santa!"

The jolly, Dominican-born pixie is the energy
15 behind "Operation Santa Claus," which makes Christmas dreams come true at the city's huge main post office, next to Penn Station and Madison Square Garden.

A record 153,000 "Dear Santa" letters from
20 around the world had arrived by Friday to be sorted, computerized and made available to anyone who wants to become an instant guardian angel. Some come from as far away as South Africa and Japan.

25 "Most post offices in the world know about us," says Colón, head of customer relations at the General Post Office.

"Operation Santa Claus" was started nearly 70 years ago by postal workers who answered
30 letters that were headed for the trash. It now attracts gifts from individuals and businesses, and is mirrored around the country at 84 other postal service consumer affairs offices.

About a third of the New York letters are "adopted." People can pick
35 through overflowing boxes to choose letters from the city's five boroughs,
as well as "Foreign," "New Jersey," "Spanish" and "Mixed States."

The opportunities don't end on Christmas. Hispanic children traditionally
receive their gifts on Epiphany in January—"El Día de Reyes," which celebrates the day the three kings brought gifts to the baby Jesus.

40 Among the letters, a New York child asks for spaghetti, rice and beans,
blankets, a coat and p.s.—"if you can"—a real live bunny.

A girl with real live mice in her Queens house asks for a mouse trap.
One child writes to "Mrs. Santa . . . because last year, I didn't get anything
from your husband."

45 Some mistake this for a lottery, like the kid who wants a cherry-red
Cadillac with matching leather interior—no convertible top, please. Some
writers attach photos of everything from pricey clothing to running shoes.

Colón, 45, who puts in hundreds of unpaid hours at work, lives with two
grown sons and a 2-year-old granddaughter. This year, they chose a letter
50 from a single mother with three children in Brooklyn and will give them
tickets for the Broadway musical "Cats."

Frank Stettner, a recording engineer, chose the note of a Florida girl
whose mother can barely pay their bills.

"To whoever you are, hope you help me get what I want, for once in a
55 lifetime," the 11-year-old wrote. "It would mean the world to me. I would
cry to get my help from you."

A portable stereo is on the way. Said Stettner, "We just want to give back
something to the world, without expecting a thank you."

Source: Associated Press

**Check Your
Comprehension**

1. What does Miracle Womack ask Santa for?

2. When did Operation Santa Claus start?

3. How does Operation Santa Claus work?

4. Why do Gigi Colón and Frank Stettner participate in Operation Santa
   Claus?

READING

Find out more about **scanning** by looking in the Reference Guide to Reading Strategies on pages xii–xiv.

Scanning

Scan the article again quickly to find the following information. Complete the following table.

1. How many post offices participate in Operation Santa Claus?

2. How many of the letters that come to New York are answered?

3. Where is New York's main post office?

4. How many boroughs are there in New York?

5. How many are mentioned in the article?

6. How many letters had arrived "by Friday"?

7. What is Epiphany?

VOCABULARY
Adjectives

Each of the adjectives in the following phrases was made from either a noun or verb. Circle the correct answer (noun or verb). Then, complete the sentence that follows, using the root noun or verb (don't use the adjective again!). The first one is done for you.

1. *pricey clothing* ((noun) verb) Pricey clothing is clothing that has a
   high price .

2. *cavernous halls* (noun verb) Cavernous halls are halls that _____ .

3. *crooked words* (noun verb) Crooked words are words that _____ .

4. *overflowing boxes* (noun verb) Overflowing boxes are boxes that
   _____ .

5. *unpaid hours* (noun verb) Unpaid hours are hours that _____ .

6. *portable stereo* (noun verb) A portable stereo is a stereo that
   _____ .

Now look through another reading in the book and find four similar phrases. Write them here.

7. _____

8. _____

9. _____

10. _____

THINK ABOUT IT

1. The two articles in this part of the chapter present different views of "neighborliness"— from Andy Rooney's view that neighbors are joined only by proximity to the Operation Santa Claus where people "adopt" strangers at Christmastime. Do these articles contradict one another? Why or why not?

2. Why do you think people participate in volunteer organizations?

3. What volunteer organizations exist in your country? Have you participated in any of them?

PART TWO

Vices: Bad Habits

How can you quit a bad habit? In this section,
the writers talk about how they quit using two addictive substances:
tobacco and heroin.

Before You Read

The Percentage of People in the United States Who Smoke, 1970–1995

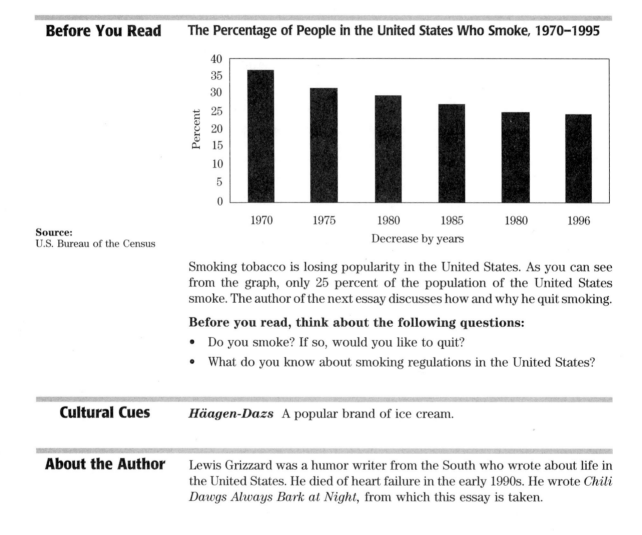

Source:
U.S. Bureau of the Census

Smoking tobacco is losing popularity in the United States. As you can see from the graph, only 25 percent of the population of the United States smoke. The author of the next essay discusses how and why he quit smoking.

Before you read, think about the following questions:

*   Do you smoke? If so, would you like to quit?
*   What do you know about smoking regulations in the United States?

Cultural Cues   *Häagen-Dazs* A popular brand of ice cream.

About the Author   Lewis Grizzard was a humor writer from the South who wrote about life in the United States. He died of heart failure in the early 1990s. He wrote *Chili Dawgs Always Bark at Night*, from which this essay is taken.

How I Quit Smoking

by Lewis Grizzard   You can't smoke anymore on New York commuter trains, and it probably won't be very long until you can't smoke anywhere.

You probably can't smoke where you work now, and restaurants and planes are becoming smoke-free.

5   What happened is the antismokers, obnoxious though they can be, have won, and smokers have become outcasts and subjects of much derision.

If you smoke, there is only one plausible thing left for you to do.

You must quit.

I know. This comes from a man who smoked his head off for years and

10   loved every cigarette he ever had.

Smoking was one of the great pleasures of my life. A cigarette was like a little reward I gave myself 25 to 40 times a day.

But I quit. For several reasons:

- I've already had two heart-valve replacement surgeries and may
15   one day face another. I need to smoke like I need getting poked in the eye with a sharp stick.

- Very few of my friends smoke anymore. I began to feel uncomfortable smoking in front of them.

- I fly 150 times a year. Airlines are turning off the smoking lights.

20   • Flying makes me nervous enough as it is without also craving a cigarette.

- None of my friends believed I really had the courage to stop smoking. I quit to prove them wrong.

Here's how I did it, after smoking for twenty-three years:

25   • I made a pact with three friends that we would stop smoking together.

- I figured at least one of them wouldn't make it and I could start again, too. But they all stayed smokeless and I hung in there with them.

- When the craving was at its worst, I kept telling myself, "Nobody
30   ever died from stopping smoking."

- I also relied on others who quit long ago who said to me, "I know it's hard for you to believe now, but there will come a time you won't even think of a cigarette anymore."

It took me three weeks to reach the point where I actually had a thought
35   other than having a cigarette.

- I substituted eating ice cream for smoking. I put on fifteen quick pounds and made the *Häagen-Dazs* people rich, but it still helped me quit smoking.

I became an obnoxious nonsmoker myself. I berated a man (a small
40 man) for lighting up in a nonsmoking area of an Amtrak train, and I bragged to friends who continued to smoke after I quit: "Well, all I can say is, I'm glad I'm no longer a slave to tobacco."

If I ever start again, I would have to face much finger-pointing and ridicule. That gives me strength to carry on.

45 I gave myself an out. I'm going to start smoking again on my ninetieth birthday.

Source: *Chili Dawgs Always Bark at Night*

Quit, dammit.

Check Your Comprehension

1. What is the current attitude toward smokers in the United States, according to the author?

2. When Grizzard became a nonsmoker, what was his attitude toward smokers?

3. How did the airlines have an influence on the author's decision to quit smoking?

READING

Find out more about **summarizing** by looking in the Reference Guide to Reading Strategies on pages xii–xiv.

Summarizing

The author uses lists to make his point. Summarize these lists by writing two paragraphs: one summarizing why he quit smoking, and one summarizing how he quit.

Why Grizzard Quit Smoking _____

_____

_____

_____

_____

_____

How Grizzard Quit Smoking _____

_____

_____

_____

_____

_____

VOCABULARY
Word Parts and Meanings

Find the following words in a dictionary that gives word parts and historical information. (The *American Heritage Dictionary* or the *Oxford English Dictionary* both give this kind of information.) Define the meaning of the part, which is underlined in each word below. Try to think of another word with the same part.

1. *obnoxious*

Meaning: _____

Another word: _____

2. *substituted*

Meaning: _____

Another word: _____

3. *commuter*

Meaning: _____

Another word: _____

4. *pact*

Meaning: _____

Another word: _____

5. *ridicule*

Meaning: _____

Another word: _____

THINK ABOUT IT

Watch the CNN video on the California smoking ban.
Discuss these questions:

1. Why did California pass a no-smoking law?

2. Why do some people dislike the law?

2. Why do some people support the law?

1. The author gives many reasons for quitting smoking. In your opinion, which is the best reason? Why?

2. The author also gives a list of things that helped him stop. Which of these do you think was probably the most effective?

3. How is smoking regarded in your culture?

4. Cigarette companies advertise heavily. Part of their strategy is to give each brand of cigarette an image. This image is meant to appeal to a certain part of the population.

Find three cigarette advertisements that you think are aimed at different parts of the population. Identify to whom each ad is trying to appeal. Do you think it is a successful ad? Why or why not?

Before You Read

New Cocaine and Heroin Users

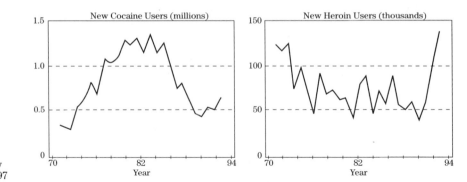

Source:
National Household Survey
on Drug Abuse, August 1997

The following account describes what it is like to be addicted to heroin, and what the author did to get rid of his addiction.

Before you read, think about the following questions:

• What kind of people do you think become heroin addicts?

• Why do you think people use drugs?

 **READING**

Find out more about **skimming** by looking in the Reference Guide to Reading Strategies on pages xii–xiv.

Skimming

Please complete this activity before you read the following article. Skim the article, taking no more than one minute. Then, in one or two sentences, write what it's about:

This article is about _____

_____

_____

_____

_____

Cultural Cues

junk Slang for heroin.

Tangier A city in northern Morocco, on the northern coast of Africa.

Scottish terrier A type of small dog.

About the Author Novelist William S. Burroughs was born in St. Louis, Missouri in 1914. He received his undergraduate degree from Harvard. He was a heroin addict for thirteen years. He wrote the famous novel, *Naked Lunch*, in 1959, which tells of some of his experiences with addiction. He died in 1997.

Kicking Drugs
A Very Personal Story

by William S. Burroughs

I was on junk for almost fifteen years. In that time I took ten cures. I have been to Lexington and have taken the reduction treatment. I have taken abrupt withdrawal treatments and 5 prolonged withdrawal treatments; cortisone, tranquilizers, antihistamines and the prolonged sleep cure. In every case I relapsed at the first opportunity.

Why do addicts voluntarily take a cure and 10 then relapse? I think on a deep biological level most addicts want to be cured.

Junk *is* death and your body knows it. I relapsed because I was never physiologically cured until 1957. Then I took the apomorphine 15 treatment under the care of a British physician, the late Dr. John Yerbury Dent. Apomorphine is the only agent I know that evicts the "addict personality," an old friend who used to inhabit my body. I call him Opium 20 Jones. We were mighty close in Tangier in 1957, shooting 15 grains of methadone every hour, which equals 30 grains of morphine and that's a lot of junk. I never changed my clothes. Jones likes his clothes to season in 25 stale rooming-house flesh until you can tell by a hat on the table, a coat hung over a chair, that Jones lives there. I never took a bath. Old Jones don't like the feel of water on his skin. I spent whole days looking at 30 the end of my shoe just communing with Jones.

Then one day I saw that Jones was not a real friend, that our interests were in fact divergent. So I took a plane to London and 35 found Dr. Dent, with a charcoal fire in the grate, Scottish terrier, cup of tea. He told me about the treatment and I entered the nursing home the following day. It was one of those four-story buildings on Cromwell Road; my room 40 with rose wallpaper was on the third floor. I had a day nurse and a night nurse and received an injection of apomorphine—one twentieth grain—every two hours.

Now every addict has his special symptom, 45 the one that hits him hardest when his junk is cut off. Listen to the old-timers in Lexington talking:

"Now with me it's puking is the worst."

"I never puke. It's this cold burn on my skin 50 drives me up the wall."

"My trouble is sneezing."

With me it's feeling the slow painful death of Mr. Jones. I feel myself encased in his old gray corpse. Not another person in this world 55 I want to see. Not a thing I want to do except revive Mr. Jones.

The third day with my cup of tea at dawn the calm miracle of apomorphine began. I was learning to live without Jones, reading news-60 papers, writing letters (usually I can't write a letter for a month), and looking forward to a talk with Dr. Dent who isn't Jones at all.

Apomorphine had taken care of my special symptom. After ten days I left the hospital.
65 During the entire cure I had received only two grains of morphine, that is, less than I had been using in one shot. I went back to Tangier, where junk was readily available at that time. I didn't have to use will power, whatever that is. I
70 just didn't want any junk. The apomorphine treatment had given me a long calm look at all the gray junk yesterdays, a long calm look at Mr. Jones standing there in his shabby black suit and gray felt hat with his stale rooming-
75 house flesh and cold undersea eyes.

Source: *Harper's Magazine*

Check Your Comprehension

1. Who is "Opium (Mr.) Jones"? What is he like?

2. What does Burroughs mean when he says that every addict has "his special symptom"? What is Burroughs' special symptom?

3. What do you think Lexington is?

VOCABULARY
Writing Definitions

Identify five words that were new to you in the reading. Write them on the following lines. Then, using the context of the reading, try to write a definition for the word. Include an example sentence, showing that you can use the word correctly in a sentence.

1. _____

_____

Example sentence: _____

2. _____

_____

Example sentence: _____

3. _____

_____

Example sentence: _____

4. _____

_____

Example sentence: _____

5. _____

_____

Example sentence: _____

THINK ABOUT IT

1. Why do you think Burroughs wrote this article?

2. Do you think the author would want drugs to be made legal?

3. What is the difference between *physiological* and *psychological* addiction? How is this difference related to Burroughs' story?

4. Finish the conversation between William S. Burroughs and "Mr. Jones."

> *Burroughs:* I am sorry, Mr. Jones, but you will have to leave.
>
> *Jones:* Why? I thought we were friends.
>
> *Burroughs:* _____
>
> *Jones:* _____
>
> *Burroughs:* _____
>
> *Jones:* _____
>
> *Burroughs:* _____

S Y N T H E S I S

Discussion and Debate

1. Many people argue that cigarette advertising should be made completely illegal. Do you agree? Do you think it would have any effect on consumer behavior?

2. Many factors contribute to drug abuse or addiction to cigarettes. What do you think is the most important cause of these problems?

3. There have been several court cases in which a tobacco company has been sued by the family of a person who died from using the product. Do you think these companies have any responsibility to the people who are harmed by their product? Why or why not?

4. "Charity begins at home," is a familiar saying. What do you think this means? How does it relate to the themes of this chapter?

5. Think of another question to ask your classmates about the material in this chapter.

Writing Topics

1. Do you have an "addiction"? To pizza, shopping, the Internet, or something else? Write a paragraph describing this "addiction," then write another paragraph proposing a way to cure it.

2. Although drug use is generally recognized as one of the greatest problems in the United States, many people feel other addictive

substances are more widespread and thus, more dangerous. Look at the following statistics:

Annual Deaths from Substance Abuse

Tobacco	346,000
Alcohol	125,000
Alcohol and Drugs	4,000
Heroin/Morphine	4,000
Cocaine	2,000
Marijuana	75

Source:" Learning and Unlearning Drug Abuse in the Real World," *Research 84*

Use these statistics, plus information from the articles in this chapter, to write a short essay about substance abuse problems in the United States.

On Your Own

1. The following films deal with alcohol or drug addiction:

   Clean and Sober   *Arthur*   *The Lost Weekend*

   Days of Wine and Roses   *Trainspotting*   *Cocaine Blues*

   Borrow any of them from your local video rental library and give a review of the film to your class.

2. Ask ten Americans the following questions, and add some questions of your own. Report your results to your class.
   - Do you think cigarette advertising should be banned?
   - Do you allow your friends to smoke in your home?
   - Do you think drugs should be legalized?
   - Do you know your neighbors?
   - Do you work for a volunteer organization?
   - Do you donate money or belongings to charity?

3. Look through some magazines and newspapers for "anti" advertising: anti-drug, anti-smoking, anti-alcohol, etc. Which of them do you think are effective? Why? Which are not? Why not? Share the advertisements with your class.

4. With a group of classmates, create an anti-smoking or anti-drug announcement for your class. It should be no longer than one or two minutes. If you can, make a videotape announcement to show your class.

★★★

A L M A N A C   For additional cultural information, refer to the Almanac on pages 221–234. The Almanac contains lists of useful facts, maps, and other information to enhance your learning.

★★★

Entertainment

The biggest U.S. export is entertainment—American films, music, and television are big business not only in the United States, but all over the world. This chapter looks at two aspects of the business of U.S. entertainment: television and sports.

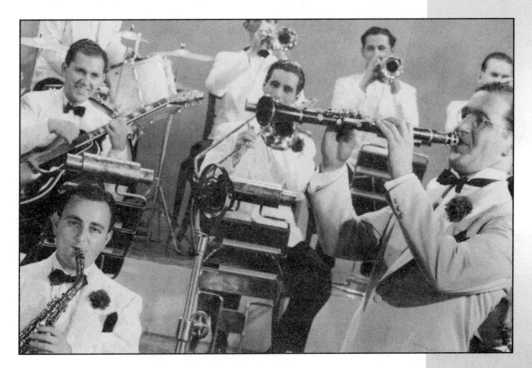

Television: The B☀☀b Tube

Television—some people love it, others hate it. One thing is clear, however; television has a big impact on American culture. Not only has television dramatically changed the public's way of receiving information, but some programs have even made a mark on American cultural history.

Before You Read

Average Hours of Television Watching per Day

	Percent of population			
Hours	1972–1982	1983–1987	1988–1991	1992–1994
0	5%	5%	3%	4%
1	19%	18%	19%	21%
2-3	45%	46%	46%	47%
4-5	21%	20.5%	21%	19%
6-10	9%	9%	9%	8%
11-15	1%	1.5%	1.5%	1%
16-20	0%	0%	0.5%	0%

Source: Adapted from the General Social Survey, 1997

Ask most Americans about television and they'll say it's awful. Yet, the average American watches it for more than two hours every day. The author of the following reading presents a theory to explain the difference between what Americans say about television, and what they actually watch.

Before you read, think about the following questions:

• Have you watched American television? Do you enjoy it?

• Do you ever feel bad about watching too much TV?

Cultural Cues

ratings The measure of the number of households that watch a particular program at a particular time; these measures are important because they determine the price of television advertising.

TV Guide A weekly magazine that contains the television schedule for each area of the United States; it also contains articles about television stars and programs.

Parcheesi A type of board game that originated in India.

About the Author   Paul L. Klein was once an executive in charge of ratings for the NBC television network. He died in 1998.

Why You Watch What You Watch When You Watch

by Paul L. Klein   It is about time that you all stop lying to each other and face up to your problems: you love television and you view too much.

I used to be the guy in charge of the ratings at NBC, and my waking hours were filled with people either complaining about how inaccurate the
5   ratings were or, without my asking them, volunteering that they "never watch TV, because the programs stink, particularly this season."

Let's look at the facts, because only by examining the nature of the disease can we cure it, or at least make peace with it.

The truth is that you buy extra sets, color sets, and even pay a monthly
10   charge for cable television to view television. Yet when you view an evening's worth of TV you are full of complaints about what you have viewed. But the next night you're right back there, hoping against hope for satisfying content, never really learning from experience, another night is shot. Instead of turning the set off and doing something else, you persist in exercising
15   the medium.

The fact is that you view TV regardless of its content. Because of the nature of the limited spectrum (only a few channels in each city) and the economic need of the networks to attract an audience large enough to attain advertising dollars which will cover the cost of production of the TV
20   program, pay the station carrying the program, and also make a profit, you are viewing programs which by necessity must appeal to the rich and poor, smart and stupid, tall and short, wild and tame, together. Therefore, you are in the vast majority of cases viewing something that is not to your taste. From the time you bought a set to now, you have viewed thousands of
25   programs which were not to your taste. The result is the hiding of, and lying about, all that viewing. Because of the hiding and lying, you are guilty. The guilt is expressed in the feeling that "I should have been reading instead of viewing."

It is of course much more difficult to read than to view. Reading requires
30   a process called *decoding*, which causes a slowdown in the information taken in by the user. TV viewing is very simple to do—kids do it better than adults because they are unencumbered by guilt—and the amount of information derived from an hour's viewing is infinitely more than is derived from an hour's reading.

35   But print has been around for a long time and it has attracted people who have learned to express themselves in this medium, so the printed

content, on the whole, is superior to the TV content. Still, most of us prefer television.

Despite the lack of quality content, the visual medium is so compelling
40 that it attracts the vast majority of adults each day to a progression of shows that most of these people would ignore in printed form.

The process of viewing works like this:

A family has just finished dinner and one member says, "Let's see what's on TV tonight." The set gets
45 turned on or the *TV Guide* gets pulled out. If it's the *TV Guide,* then the list of programs (most of which are repeats) is so unappealing that each member of the family says to himself that he remembers when *TV Guide* made an awful error in its program listings back
50 in 1967 and maybe it has happened again.

The set is turned on whether a good program is listed or not at that time. Chances are 100 to 1 that there is nothing on that meets this or any family's taste for that moment. But the medium meets their taste.

55 The viewer(s) then slowly turns the channel selector, grumbling at each image he sees on the screen. Perhaps he'll go around the dial two or three times before settling on one channel whose program is *least objectionable.*

60 "Well, let's watch this," someone in the family says. "There's nothing better on." So they watch. No one thinks of jogging a couple of laps around the block or getting out the old Parcheesi board. They watch whatever is least objectionable.

65 The programmers for the networks have argued that this is a "most satisfying" choice—not LOP (least objectionable program). But if it were, then why would everybody be complaining and lying about TV viewing? I don't deny that in some rare time periods, "least objectionable" is actually most satisfying, but the bulk of the time people are
70 viewing programs they don't particularly consider good, and that is why the medium is so powerful and rich.

Source: *TV Guide*

Check Your Comprehension

1. Why aren't there television programs that suit most people's individual tastes?

2. Why does Klein think that people feel guilty about watching television? What is the result of this guilt?

3. What is Klein's theory of "least objectionable program"? Do you agree with his theory?

READING

Find out more about **understanding point of view** by looking in the Reference Guide to Reading Strategies on pages xii–xiv.

Understanding Point of View

Fill in the following information about the author of "Why You Watch. . . ."

Gender: _____

Job: _____

Now, summarize the author's point of view. Write one paragraph describing the main point(s) of the article:

_____

_____

_____

_____

_____

_____

How do you think the author's background might influence his point of view about the subject matter?

VOCABULARY
Colloquial Language

Use each of the following colloquial phrases correctly in a sentence.

1. *it's about time*

    _____

    _____

2. *it stinks*

    _____

    _____

3. *hoping against hope*

    _____

    _____

4. *another night is shot*

    _____

    _____

5. *on the whole*

    _____

    _____

THINK ABOUT IT

1. Although the article was written in the early 1970s, it is still relevant today. What clues in the reading tell you that it is an older article?

2. Klein mentions that people feel guilty because they don't read more. Has television had an effect on your own reading habits? As a child, did you prefer reading or watching TV?

3. The author states that there are times when nothing is on that meets a family's taste, but the "medium meets their taste." What does this mean? Have you ever felt that way?

4. There are reports that the Internet is decreasing the amount of time Americans spend watching television. Do you spend less time watching television because of the Internet?

Before You Read

Ten Television Firsts

The first regular television program service in the world.	1935, in Berlin, Germany
The first American President to appear on television	Franklin D. Roosevelt, April 30, 1939
The first televised professional baseball game	Brooklyn Dodgers versus Philadelphia Eagles, at Ebbets Field, Brooklyn, New York, August 26, 1939
The first color television programs were tested in the United States	1941
The first television commercial	1941, a 10-second commercial for Bulova clocks
First broadcast of a current U.S. television program	*Meet the Press*, NBC, November 6, 1947
Color television introduced in the United States	1953
The first soap opera on television	February 21, 1947, *A Woman to Remember*
First filmed U.S. presidential news conference	January 19, 1955 with Dwight D. Eisenhower
First live U.S. presidential news conference	Jan 25, 1961, John F. Kennedy

The next reading, an article from an online series, tells about Philo T. Farnsworth, one of the American inventors behind television.

Before you read, think about the following questions:
- How much do you know about television's history?
- Were you taught about the history of television in any history class?

Cultural Cues

Brigham Young The second president of the Mormon Church.

Jules Vernian Referring to Jules Verne, the French writer known as the "father of science fiction".

About the Author

Paul Schatzkin writes installments of "The Farnsworth Chronicles" on the Internet. He is also the president of the National Online Music Alliance, a Nashville-based organization dedicated to the promotion of independent musicians on the Internet.

The Farnsworth Chronicles
by Paul Schatzkin

The story of television begins in Rigby, Idaho in the spring of 1919, as a small wagon train reaches the crest of a hill overlooking a humble, turn-of-the-century homestead. The family of
5 Lewis and Serena Farnsworth has arrived at their new home, after an arduous journey over the mountains from their native Utah.

Seated at the reins of one of the three covered wagons was the oldest child, Philo, age
10 11 and named after his grandfather, who came west with Brigham Young. As the boy surveyed the scene before him he noticed one detail which the rest of the family missed: on the farm below, he could see wires running between the
15 different buildings and shouted excitedly, "This place has electricity!"

With this discovery, the family left the ridge and began their descent into a new life on the frontier of the Twentieth Century. Little Philo
20 was about to come face-to-face for the first time with the mysterious force he had only read about in books, that invisible power that could drive great machines and turn darkness into light. Though he was about to encounter

25 electricity for the first time at age 11, he would prove to be one of the great masters of that mysterious force before he was 21.

A few weeks after his arrival in Rigby, Philo had figured out all by himself what made the
30 electrical system work. Lewis Farnsworth realized that his son had a natural affinity for the system when Philo stepped in one day to repair the disabled generator while all the adults stood around wondering what had gone wrong.
35 Thus, the boy-electrician became officially installed as the chief engineer of the Farnsworth farm, and the electrical system became his own very special domain.

With encouragement from his father, Philo
40 found a dozen new uses for his invisible friend. He built motors from spare parts and used them to run his mother's washing machine and some of the farm machines. The time he saved by automating these chores he spent thinking about
45 better things. In the attic above the house, Philo created his own world to explore electricity in whatever books or journals his father could afford. The loft became his hideaway, where

with each succeeding page, his imagination was
50 fired by stories of science and the modern day
sorcerers who unraveled its mysteries. To Philo,
inventors of all kinds seemed to possess a special power that allowed them to see deep into
the mysteries of nature and use her secrets to
55 ease the burden for all mankind. He confided in
his father his own heart's desire: that he, too,
had been born an inventor.

In the fall of 1921, Philo entered high school
as a freshman but soon found the material too
60 dull and cajoled his way into the senior chemistry class. When even that advanced course
proved inadequate for the youngster's thirst,
the chemistry teacher, a bespectacled and
slightly past middle-age gentleman named Jus-
65 tin Tolman, took extra time after class each day
to tutor his young prodigy. It became quickly
apparent to Tolman that he was tutoring perhaps the smartest student he would ever meet
in his life.

70 One cold night in January, 1922, Philo was
particularly anxious to finish his chores after
school and hurry back to the books and magazines in his attic hideaway. As he turned the
pages, he stumbled upon an article about some-
75 thing very new: "Pictures That Could Fly
Through the Air." The writer described an electronic magic carpet, a marriage of
radio and movies, that would carry
far-off worlds into the home in simul-
80 taneous sight and sound. Philo was
instantly captivated by the idea. He
reread the article several times,
convinced that he had stumbled onto
a problem that he was uniquely
85 equipped to solve.

When Philo determined to learn
everything he could about the subject,
he stepped into a Jules-Vernian world
where scientists were trying to con-
90 vert light into electricity with the aid
of whirling discs and mirrors. Farnsworth realized right away that those
discs and mirrors would never whirl
fast enough to transmit a coherent

95 image, and searched for a device that could
travel at the speed of light itself. He found the
solution in his invisible new friend, the electron.

While the great minds of science, financed
by the biggest companies in the world, wrestled
100 with 19th century answers to a 20th century
problem, Philo T. Farnsworth, age 13, was
chained to a horse-drawn harvesting machine,
crisscrossing the fields endlessly, row by row,
harvesting the crops and dreaming about tele-
105 vision to relieve the monotony. As the open
summer sun blazed down on him, a daring idea
fermented in this boy's brain: He dreamed of
trapping light in an empty jar and transmitting
it one-line-at-a-time on a magnetically deflected
110 beam of electrons.

This principle still forms the heart of modern television. Though the essence of the idea
is extraordinarily simple, it eluded the most
prominent scientists of the day. Yet here it had
115 crystallized in the mind of a 13-year-old boy.

It seems quite unlikely that an unknown
boy with little education, no money, and no
equipment could steal the race from the greatest electrical companies in the world, but that
120 is precisely what Farnsworth set out to do. His
father advised Philo not to discuss his idea with
anyone. Ideas, he reasoned, were too valuable

and fragile, and could be pirated easily. But Philo had to talk to someone, he needed to
125 hear from somebody besides his father that his idea would work.

Late one afternoon in March of 1922, Justin Tolman was startled to see a complicated array of electrical diagrams scattered across the
130 blackboard in his classroom. At the front of the room stood his gangling young prodigy, chalking in the last few figures of the last equation and turning to his teacher.

"What has this got to do with Chemistry?"
135 Tolman asked.

"I've got this idea," Farnsworth calmly replied. "I've got to tell you about it because you're the only person I know who can understand it." The boy paused and took a deep breath. "This is
140 my idea for electronic television."

"Television?" Tolman said, "What's that?"

Source: The National Online Music Alliance

Check Your Comprehension

1. Who was Philo Farnsworth?

2. How did Philo's father discover Philo had a talent for understanding electricity?

3. Why did Philo's father tell him not to discuss his ideas with anyone?

4. What is the principle behind modern television?

READING

Find out more about **understanding processes** by looking in the Reference Guide to Reading Strategies on pages xii–xiv.

Understanding Processes

The "Farnsworth Chronicles" tells the story of an historical **process**. Review the story, and put the following events into proper order. Write a date next to each event. (Hint: Some dates are not available, others you may have to do some math to solve.) The first one is done for you.

Date	Order	Event
		Justin Tolman agrees to tutor Philo after school.
		Justin Tolman discovers Philo's equations.
		Philo becomes one of the "masters of the mysterious force."
		Philo enters high school as a freshman.
		Philo reads the article, "Pictures That Could Fly Through the Air."
unknown; years before the main story	1	Philo's grandfather comes to Utah with Brigham Young.
		The Lewis and Serena Farnsworth family reaches their new home in Utah.

VOCABULARY
Understanding Synonyms

This article has several words that may have been new to you. Choose a synonym for each. Draw a line to the correct synonym.

1. source of power
2. string of carriages
3. wearing glasses
4. unexplored periphery
5. sameness
6. particle in an atom
7. magician
8. field
9. divert
10. difficult
11. persuade
12. child genius
13. attraction

a. affinity
b. arduous
c. bespectacled
d. cajole
e. deflect
f. domain
g. electron
h. frontier
i. generator
j. monotony
k. prodigy
l. sorcerer
m. wagon train

THINK ABOUT IT

1. Farnsworth's story has been called a "typically American" tale. Why do you think this is so?

2. Do you think the invention of television was a good thing? Why or why not?

3. Imagine a world without television. How would daily life be different?

PART TWO

Sprts: Play Ball

Sports is an important part of American entertainment and culture. Professional football, baseball, and basketball all have large audiences, both on television and in the stadiums. Among the other sports that enjoy great popularity in America are soccer, tennis, golf, gymnastics . . . the list is long.

Before You Read   **A Standard Baseball Diamond**

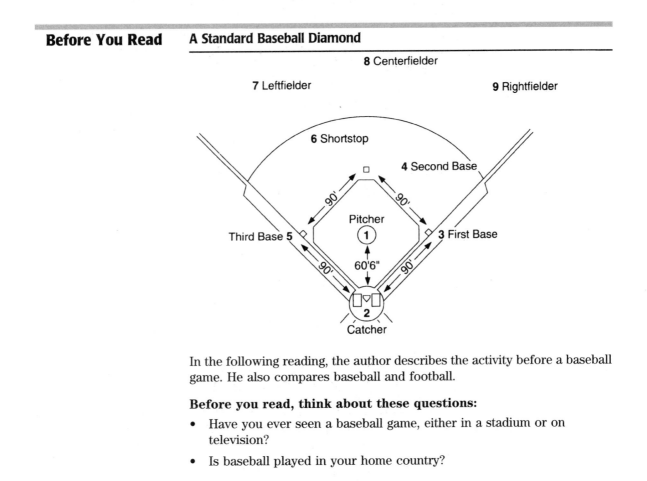

In the following reading, the author describes the activity before a baseball game. He also compares baseball and football.

Before you read, think about these questions:

- Have you ever seen a baseball game, either in a stadium or on television?

- Is baseball played in your home country?

Cultural Cues   ***pepper*** A throwing exercise in which the players throw the ball around the field quickly.

batting cage The metal frame that is placed behind home plate during

169

batting practice; it keeps the balls from being hit into the stands, where the spectators sit.

dugout The enclosure where the players' bench is; it is called a *dugout* because many of them are actually dug into the ground.

clubhouse The area in a ballpark that contains a locker room, showers, and offices; each ballpark has two clubhouses, one for the home team and one for the visiting team.

innings The portion of a baseball game during which each team gets a chance to score; there are nine innings in a baseball game. If at the end of nine innings the scores are tied, more innings are played until someone wins.

baserunner The player who, after hitting the ball, has succeeded in reaching one of the bases but has not yet returned to home plate.

home plate Spot on the field where the players bat; the base runners must cross home plate in order to score.

umpire The official who serves as judge during the game; there are typically four umpires on the field during the game.

catcher The player behind home plate who catches the balls the pitcher throws.

pitcher The player who stands in the middle of the diamond and throws the ball to the batter; the batter in order to score a run, makes a complete circuit of all the bases.

"Take Me Out To the Ball Game" The most popular baseball song, often sung during ballgames by the spectators.

About the Author   Mike Whiteford is a sportswriter for the *Charleston Gazette*, a newspaper published in the city of Charleston, West Virginia.

Baseball by Mike Whiteford

The first hints of baseball's distinction as a gentle, lighthearted affair emerge long before game time. The players are scattered about, busying themselves in conversation, autograph-signing, playing catch or pepper in front of the dugout or cards in the clubhouse. During BP—batting practice for the uniniti-
5   ated—the players cluster around the batting cage where laughter and extravagant smiles abound, reflecting the banter that accompanies this pre-game ritual.

By contrast, football players devote their pre-game hours to trying to

arouse themselves into frenzied hostility. They pound on lockers and each
10 other. The coaches grimly review the game plan one more time. At a pre-
determined moment, often specified by a television director, the players
trudge from the locker room through a tunnel, ceremoniously onto the field,
accompanied by the sounds of bands, cheerleaders, and a raucous crowd.

As game time approaches in baseball, the guys wend their way unhur-
15 riedly to their appropriate places on the bench. A more forward player might
find a spot slightly to the side of the dugout, making himself more visible
to the fans. A crew of relief pitchers and extra catchers shuffles off for the
bullpen. At the appropriate moment the starting nine jog onto the field and
stir polite applause among the spectators.

20 At most ballparks, an organist, already having played "Take Me Out to
the Ball Game" and other familiar favorites, grinds out the national anthem.
Then the game commences, though many of the fans are still settling into
their seats or gazing around the ballpark. It's considerably different, of
course, at the start of a football game. All 50,000 fans are on their feet
25 screaming. It's tradition, you understand.

Once under way, baseball offers a leisurely, relaxed pace, giving the
fans, reporters, broadcasters, and players plenty of time to ponder the
proceedings, exercise their imaginations, and allow their minds to wander.

Baseball drama is at its best in the late innings, perhaps the eighth, with
30 the score tied or with one team leading by a run. Base-runners dance off
first and second, trying to unnerve the pitcher, who peers at them through
the corner of his eye. The pitcher then leans toward home plate, squints
and stares interminably as the batter menacingly wigwags his bat. Finally,
after glancing at the runners one more time, the pitcher delivers, the umpire
35 bellows strike two, the entire routine is repeated and the drama continues
to build.

Except in rare instances, nothing happens at a baseball game that reaches
out and grabs the spectator or shouts at him; it only beckons to him alluringly
as he reflects on and considers the possibilities.

**Check Your
Comprehension**

1. Describe the difference between pre-game activities in baseball and
    football.

2. When is baseball most exciting, according to the author?

3. What does the author like about baseball's slow pace?

READING

Find out more about **understanding processes** by looking in the Reference Guide to Reading Strategies on pages xii–xiv.

Understanding Processes

This reading describes a process. However, the author uses a lot of *descriptive* words. Explain the process of a baseball game, as described by the author, but use only the *facts*, not his colorful descriptions. The paragraph is started for you.

> *First, before the game, the players . . .* _____

_____

_____

_____

_____

VOCABULARY
Descriptive Words

The sixteen verbs below are more descriptive than the more typical verbs that are normally used. Look at the following verbs, and look them up if you don't understand them. Then, answer the questions that follow.

banter	*dance*	*ponder*	*stare*
beckon	*gaze*	*reflect*	*trudge*
bellow	*jog*	*shuffle*	*wander*
cluster	*peer*	*squint*	*wend*

1. Which of these verbs are ways of moving?

_____

2. Which are ways of thinking?

_____

3. Which are ways of looking?

_____

4. Which are ways of speaking?

_____

5. Which are ways of doing activities slowly?

_____

6. Which are ways of doing activities quickly?

_____

7. Which are ways of doing something loudly?

_____

8. Which are ways of doing something quietly?

_____

THINK ABOUT IT

1. Do you think the author prefers baseball or football? What clues are there in the reading?

2. Sports are often said to reflect the "national character" of a country. In the United States, some say that football is the national game, while others say it is baseball. Which game do you think reflects the "national character" of the United States better? Why?

3. The figures below are part of the "box scores," a part of the sports pages in newspapers that tell how all the baseball teams played the day before. These box scores show the statistics of two games.

Cubs 5, Cardinals 3

ST. LOUIS	ab	r	h	bi	CHICAGO	ab	r	h	bi
MThompson rf	5	1	1	0	Walton cf	4	3	2	0
OSmith ss	4	0	0	0	Sandberg 2b	4	1	2	2
McGee cf	4	0	1	0	Grace 1b	3	0	1	2
Guerrero 1b	3	0	1	1	Dawson rf	4	0	0	0
Zeile c	3	1	0	0	DClark lf	4	0	0	0
Pendleton 3b	4	0	1	0	MiWilliams p	0	0	0	0
Hudler lf	3	1	1	1	Salazar 3b	4	1	3	0
Oquendo 2b	3	0	2	1	Dunston ss	4	0	1	1
Tewksbury p	2	0	0	0	Girardi c	3	0	0	0
Coleman ph	0	0	0	0	Bielecki p	2	0	1	0
Terry p	0	0	0	0	Assenmchr p	0	0	0	0
CWilson ph	1	0	0	0	Varsho ph	1	0	0	0
					Long p	0	0	0	0
					Wynne lf	0	0	0	0
Totals	**32**	**3**	**7**	**3**	**Totals**	**33**	**5**	**10**	**5**

St. Louis	011	000	100—3
Chicago	101	001	20x—5

Reds 1, Dodgers 0

LOS ANGELES	ab	r	h	bi	CINNINNATI	ab	r	h	bi
Sharperson 2b	4	0	0	0	Larkin ss	3	0	0	0
Gibson cf	4	0	2	0	ONeill rf	3	0	2	0
Daniels lf	4	0	1	0	Sabo 3b	3	0	0	0
Murray 1b	4	0	2	0	EDavis cf	3	0	0	0
Brooks rf	4	0	1	0	HMorris 1b	3	0	0	0
MHatcher 3b	3	0	0	0	Duncan 2b	3	0	0	0
LHarris 2b	0	0	0	0	Oliver c	3	0	0	0
Dempsey c	4	0	0	0	BHatcher lf	3	1	0	0
Crews p	0	0	0	0	Browning p	2	0	0	0
Griffin ss	4	0	2	0	Myers p	0	0	0	0
Neidlinger p	3	0	0	0					
Searage p	0	0	0	0					
Scioscia c	1	0	0	0					
Totals	**35**	**0**	**8**	**0**	**Totals**	**26**	**1**	**2**	**0**

Los Angeles	000	000	100	0
Cinninnati	000	000	01x—1	

Symbols heading the columns of numbers:

ab = at bat; the number of times the player had a turn trying to hit the ball

r = run; the number of times the player successfully hit the ball and ran all the way around the bases, scoring a point

h = hit; the number of times the player hit the ball

bi = batted in; the number of players that scored because the player at bat hit the ball

Symbols for positions on the field:

p = pitcher

ss = short stop

lf = left fielder

cf = center fielder

rf = right fielder

ph = pinch hitter (a batter who is sent into the game to bat for another batter)

c = catcher

$1b$ = first baseman

$2b$ = second baseman

$3b$ = third baseman

The summary at the bottom of the chart shows the number of runs scored in each inning. The x in the last place among the numbers for the Chicago team shows that the second half of the last inning was not played because they had already won the game.

a. Who won the game between Los Angeles and Cincinnati?

_____

b. Who lost the game between St. Louis and Chicago?

_____

c. Which players were never at bat?

_____

d. Which player was at bat the most?

_____

e. Which player hit the most runs? What position does he play?

_____

f. Which player got three hits? What position does he play?

_____

g. Which players had the most "batted ins"?

_____

h. Who were the first catchers who played in the two games?

_____

i. How many pitchers played in the two games? Who were they?

_____

j. In which game did both teams score in the third inning?

_____

k. In which game and inning were three runs scored?

_____

l. What was the total score in the fourth inning of both games?

_____

Before You Read

Professional wrestlers

In the following reading, the author describes and explains the sport of professional wrestling. (This reading has many idioms and less common words. As you read, keep focusing on the main point, and don't worry about looking up every word.)

Before you read, think about the following questions:

- Have you ever seen professional wrestling, either on television or in person? What was it like?

- What sports do you enjoy watching?

Cultural Cues

draft card A card given to American men in the past, indicating their eligibility to serve in the military forces. The draft is not currently active in the United States.

Harlem A primarily African-American neighborhood in New York City with a rich history.

Lenox Avenue & 125th Street Intersection in the heart of Harlem.

linebacker A position on an American football team.

Jets A New York football team.

NCAA National Collegiate Athletic Association.

Choctaw A native American nation.

turnbuckle A metal fastener that is part of a wrestling ring.

FRIDAY NIGHT AT THE COLISEUM
BY WILLIAM C. MARTIN

Pro wrestling has been part of the American scene for more than a century and has enjoyed several periods of wide popularity. For most fans over thirty, however, it began sometime
5 around 1949, with the arrival of television. Lou Thesz was world champion in those days, but the man who symbolized professional wrestling to most people was Gorgeous George, a consummate exhibitionist whose long golden
10 curls, brocade and satin robes, and outrageously effeminate manner drew huge crowds wherever he went, all hoping to see a local he-man give him the beating he so obviously deserved.

15 The Gorgeous One's success at the box office ushered in a new era of wrestler, each trying to appear more outrageous than the others. For many, villainy showman has provided the surest route to fame and fortune. The over-
20 whelming majority of professional wrestling matches pit the Good, the Pure, and the True against the Bad, the Mean, and the Ugly, and a man with a flair for provoking anger and hatred has an assured future in the sport. Since
25 shortly after World War II, the most dependable source of high displeasure has been the Foreign Menace, usually an unreconstructed Nazi or a wily Japanese who insults the memory of our boys in uniform with actions so contemptu-
30 ous one cannot fail to be proud that our side won the war.

Wrestling fans are generally an egalitarian lot, at least among themselves, and they do not appreciate those who put on airs. So they are
35 easily angered by another strain of crowd displeaser one might call Titled Snobs and Pointy-Headed Intellectuals. These villains, who love to call themselves "Professor" or "Doctor" or "Lord" Somebody-or-other, use the standard

40 bag of tricks —pulling a man down by his hair, rubbing his eyes with objects secreted in trunks or shoes, stomping his face while he lies wounded and helpless —but their real specialty is treating the fans like ignorant yahoos.
45 They walk and speak with disdain for common folk, and never miss a chance to belittle the crowd in sesquipedalian put-downs or to declare that their raucous and uncouth behavior calls for nothing less than a letter to the *Times*,
50 to inform proper Englishmen of the deplorable state of manners in the Colonies.

A third prominent villain is the Big Mean Son of a Gun. Dick the Bruiser, Cowboy Bill Watts, Butcher Vachone, Killer Kowalski—
55 these men do not need swastikas and monocles and big words to make you hate them. They have the bile of human meanness by the quart in every vein. If a guileless child hands a Sonofabitch a program to autograph, he will
60 often brush it aside or tear it into pieces and throw it on the floor. It isn't that he has forgotten what it was like to be a child. As a child, he kicked crutches from under crippled newsboys and cheated on tests and smoked in the rest
65 room. Now, at 260 pounds, he goes into the ring not just to win, but to injure and maim. Even before the match begins, he attacks his trusting opponent from behind, pounding his head into the turnbuckle, kicking him in the
70 kidneys, stomping him in the groin, and generally seeking to put him at a disadvantage. These are bad people. None of us is really safe as long as they go unpunished.

Fortunately, these hellish legions do not
75 hold sway unchallenged by the forces of Right. For every villain there is a hero who seeks to hold his own against what seem to be incredible odds. Heroes also fall into identifiable cate-

gories. Most of them are trim and handsome
80 young men in their twenties or early thirties,
the sort that little boys want to grow up to be,
and men want to have as friends, and women
want to have, also. Personable Bobby Shane
wins hearts when he wrestles in his red, white,
85 and blue muscle suit with the "USA" mono-
gram: and when Tim Woods, dressed all in
white, is introduced as a graduate of Michigan
State University, older folk nod approvingly.
They want their sons and grandsons to go to
90 college, even though they didn't have a chance
to go themselves, and it is reassuring to see
living proof that not everybody who goes to
college is out burning draft cards and blowing
up banks.

95   Though quick to capitalize on the jingoist
appeal of matches involving Menacing Foreigners, few promoters will risk a match that might
divide the house along racial lines. So black
and brown wrestlers usually appear in the role
100 of Hero, behind whom virtually the entire
crowd can unite. Browns—Mexicans, Mexican-
Americans, and Puerto Ricans—are almost in-
variably handsome, lithe, and acrobatic. They
fight "scientifically" and seldom resort to
105 roughhouse tactics until they have endured so
much that the legendary Latin temper can no
longer be contained. If a black chooses to play
the villain, he will soften the racial element:
when Buster Lloyd, the Harlem Hangman,
110 came into town, he belittled the skills of his
opponents not because they were white, but
because they were Texans and therefore little
challenge for a man who learned to fight at the
corner of Lenox Avenue and 125th Street.
115 Several white grapplers might have been able

to handle Buster, but the hero selected to take
his measure and send him packing back to Harlem was Tiger Conway, a black Texan.

The purest of pure Americans, of course,
120 and a people well acquainted with villainy, are
Red Indians. Most wrestling circuits feature a
Red Indian from time to time; in Houston, ex-
Jets linebacker Chief Wahoo McDaniel is the
top attraction and has wrestled in the Coliseum
125 more than a hundred times in the last three
years. Like Chief White Owl, Chief Suni War
Cloud, and Chief Billy Two Rivers, Wahoo en-
ters the ring in moccasin-style boots, warbon-
net, and other Indian authentica. He can endure
130 great pain and injustice without flinching or
retaliating in kind, but when enraged, or sometimes just to get the old adrenaline going, he
will rip into a furious war dance and level his
opponent with a series of karate-like Toma-
135 hawk Chops to the chest or scalp, then force
him into submission with the dreaded Choctaw
Death Lock.

The Portrayal of Life that unfolds in the
ring is no naïve melodrama in which virtue
140 always triumphs and cheaters never win. Whatever else these folk know, they know that life
is tough and filled with conflict, hostility, and
frustration. For every man who presses toward
the prize with pure heart and clean hands, a
145 dozen Foreigners and so-called Intellectuals
and Sonsofbitches seek to bring him down with
treachery and brute force and outright meanness. And even if he overcomes these, there
are other, basically decent men who seek to
150 defeat him in open competition.

Source: Excerpted from: "Friday Night in the Coliseum"
The Atlantic Monthly

**Check Your
Comprehension**

1. How long has professional wrestling been around, according to the
    article?

2. What is meant by the phrase "the Foreign Menace"?

3. Why do "black and brown" wrestlers usually play the role of Hero,
    according to the author?

4. How did Gorgeous George symbolize professional wrestling?

READING

Find out more about **understanding by categorizing** by looking in the Reference Guide to Reading Strategies on pages xii–xiv.

Understanding by Categorizing

In this article, the author categorizes wrestlers by type. Summarize the categories and examples he gives. Use the following outline form.

Categories of Wrestlers

Wrestler Type 1: _____

    Example 1: _____

    Example 2: _____

    Example 3: _____

Wrestler Type 2: _____

    Example 1: _____

    Example 2: _____

    Example 3: _____

Review this outline, then write the conclusion of the article in your own words.

_____

_____

_____

_____

VOCABULARY
Idiomatic Phrases

This article has a lot of idiomatic phrases. Look at the following idiomatic phrases and review the reading to see if you can determine what they mean. Then, put the letter of the definition that most closely matches the meaning before each phrase.

__j__	**1.** an egalitarian lot	**a.**	act sophisticated
_____	**2.** brute force	**b.**	average people
_____	**3.** common folk	**c.**	become excited
_____	**4.** get the adrenaline going	**d.**	frightening crowds
_____	**5.** hellish legions	**e.**	have influence
_____	**6.** he-man	**f.**	insult
_____	**7.** hold one's own	**g.**	intellectual
_____	**8.** hold sway	**h.**	maintain one's position
_____	**9.** ignorant yahoo	**i.**	masculine person

_____ **10.** pointy-headed √ **j.** people who don't discriminate

_____ **11.** put-down **k.** raw strength

_____ **12.** put on airs **l.** stupid person

_____ **13.** Titled Snobs **m.** wealthy, self-important people

_____ **14.** usher in **n.** welcome

THINK ABOUT IT

1. What is the purpose of professional wrestling, according to this article?

2. Although wrestlers fall into categories, according to the author, the owners are careful to avoid the divisions being racial. Why do you think this is so? What would be the consequences if the divisions were racially motivated?

3. Watch a professional wrestling match on television. How do current wrestlers fall into the categories talked about in this article? Do you observe any new categories?

4. Is professional wrestling popular in your country? How does it compare to American professional wrestling?

SYNTHESIS

Discussion and Debate

 Watch the CNN video on funny women of television.
Discuss these questions:
1. Who are some of the famous funny women of television?
2. Who are your favorite television comedians?

1. Many people feel that entertainers of all kinds (including athletes) are paid too much. How do you feel about this issue?

2. Some people are proud that they do not watch television or sporting events. Others say you can't really understand a culture without knowing its entertainment. What do you think?

3. Is the idea of entertainment the same in your culture as in U.S. culture? What are the important similarities and differences?

4. Sports teams and other entertainment organizations participate in "merchandising" themselves or their creations. For example, they sell products like T-shirts with team names or television characters on them. Have you ever purchased any of this type of merchandise? Why or why not?

5. What forms of entertainment do you most enjoy?

6. Think of another question to ask your classmates about the ideas in this chapter.

Writing Topics   1. Investigate a U.S. sport which you would like to know more about. Read about it and write a report with the following general outline:
a. Brief history of the game
b. Description of the rules
c. Current state of the game (important players, teams, or prizes)
Make an oral report to your class and include visual aids, such as photographs or charts.

2. Look up two or more reviews of a movie on the Internet or in newspapers. Write a report in which you compare the opinion of the reviewers. If you've seen the movie, also discuss your opinion.

3. Write a letter to a friend back home describing how you spent your last "free" day—a day during which you didn't work or study, but did the things you wanted to do. (If you haven't had such a day recently, write about how you would like to spend such a day.)

On Your Own   1. Find a story in the sports pages of the newspaper that interests you. Read it and summarize the story for your classmates.

2. Survey ten people about their leisure time. Ask them the following questions, in addition to your own.

   • Do you participate in any sports? Which ones?
   • Do you watch sports on television? Which ones?
   • How much television do you watch in one day?
   • What is your favorite television show?
   • What was your favorite television show ten years ago?

   Summarize your results and compare them with those of your classmates.

3. There is a one-in-four chance that an American has been on television. Try to find someone who has been on TV (or in a movie of any type). Ask that person about his or her experience. If you have been on TV, describe to your classmates what it was like.

★★

A L M A N A C   For additional cultural information, refer to the Almanac on pages 221–234. The Almanac contains lists of useful facts, maps, and other information to enhance your learning.

★★★

Technology

Technology is advancing at a rapid pace. The introduction of the Internet, e-mail, and other technological advances is rapidly changing the way Americans communicate. Many see it as a revolution in modern culture.

PART ONE

Computers; Making Connections

Computers are, of course, the most important part of recent
advances in technology. Computers used to exist only in universities and laboratories—now
they are on nearly everyone's desk.

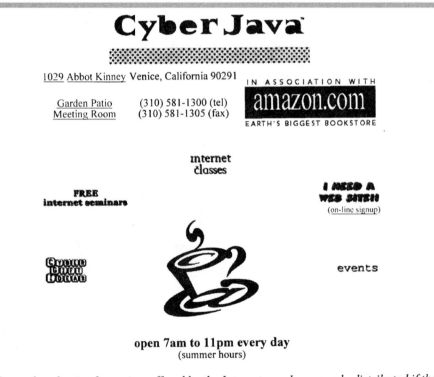

Cyber Java

1029 Abbot Kinney Venice, California 90291

Garden Patio
Meeting Room

(310) 581-1300 (tel)
(310) 581-1305 (fax)

IN ASSOCIATION WITH

amazon.com
EARTH'S BIGGEST BOOKSTORE

internet
classes

FREE
internet seminars

I NEED A
WEB SITE!!
(on-line signup)

events

open 7am to 11pm every day
(summer hours)

*"The profound gains for society offered by the Internet may be unevenly distributed if the
large population without knowledge or access to computers are left out of Cyberspace.
Promises of a 'global village' and 'digital democracy' may be unfulfilled if computers
remain the exclusive tool of the specially educated or affluent. Cyber Java's mission is to
bring Internet education and connectivity to coffee drinkers everywhere!"*

--Cyber Java Manifesto--

Cyber Java's (an Internet café) homepage, http://www.cyberjava.com/

Before You Read

In this article, the author talks about "cybercafés," places where people can go to drink coffee and to connect to the Internet. This article was written for a newspaper, so its paragraphs are shorter than you would find in a standard essay.

Before you read, think about the following questions:

- Do you know if your city has a cybercafé?
- Have you ever visited a cybercafé?

Cultural Cues

latte A type of coffee drink which has a lot of milk and strong espresso coffee.

Sartre Jean-Paul Sartre, a twentieth century French novelist.

Hemingway Ernest Hemingway, a twentieth century American novelist.

Beat poet Poets of the 1950s and early 1960s such as William Burroughs and Allen Ginsburg; they were known as the "Beat" generation, which is short for "beatniks".

America Online The largest Internet service provider in the United States.

REDEFINING CAFÉ SOCIETY, ONLINE

by Amy Harmon

Sometime around early 1995, America's respective infatuations with coffee and cyberspace collided to form an improbable new hybrid called the cybercafé.

Suddenly, before you could double-click on a double latte, they were
5 everywhere, from the Octane Interlounge in Rockford, Ill., to the IDT Megabite Café in midtown Manhattan, hawking computerized caféculture for $10–$15 an hour.

To many, the premise seemed inherently flawed—not to mention a crude bastardization of a caffeinated icon heretofore associated with Sartre, Hem-
10 ingway and the Beat poets. Cafés are supposed to be about communication and counterculture. Why would anyone go to one to stare into a computer screen? And what would it mean if they did?

But without getting overly existential about it, the success of the cybercafé does raise the question of just what community means at a time when
15 literature is composed on laptops and revolution (or whatever) can be just as easily debated with comrades sipping espresso thousands of miles away.

Except to check e-mail on the road, the digital elite have largely boycotted the digital coffeehouse. "I sit in front of a computer 12 hours a day," said

Jason McCabe Calacanis, editor of *The Silicon Alley Reporter.* "Do you
20 really think I'd go sit in front of one to relax?"

Kit Galloway, a founder of the Electronic Café in Santa Monica, Calif.,
which opened in 1988, before the concept became trendy, derides many of
the newcomers as "cybermats."

On a recent late evening at the Cyber Café in downtown Manhattan, two
25 young men sat at separate computer terminals entirely entwined in the
psychic combat of the networked game Quake.

Meanwhile, at the Internet Café in the East Village, Sara Pasquinelli
surfed for travel tips on Spain as her friend listened to the live jazz band.
A few blocks away at Alt.Coffee, Yaakov Shapiro gulped an iced coffee with
30 milk as he logged onto the Judaism discussion on America Online. "I'm
trying to set straight the atheists and the evolutionists," he explained.

And Colleen Werthmann, 26, an actress, spent 20 minutes intently typing
her response to an e-mail discussion on jungle music vs. hip-hop unfolding
somewhere in the ether.

35 "I come here to post," said Ms. Werthmann, who does not own a computer
and taught herself how to use the Internet two months ago at a temporary
job. "Do I talk to all these other people? No. That's what's good about it.
You don't have to engage in some kind of bogus conversation about yoga
or pretend to be interested in somebody's band."

40 Still, it is the other people who account for the majority of Alt.Coffee's
patrons.

"This is like our living room," said Joy Magyawe, 19, ensconced with a
friend on a low-slung couch drinking plain coffee. "But we never use the
computers."

Source: The *New York Times:* "Cybertimes"

Check Your Comprehension

1. The author claims that the cybercafé is the combination of two
    interests. What are they?

2. Why do some people dislike cybercafés?

3. Why do others like the cybercafés?

READING

Find out more about **understanding definitions** by looking in the Reference Guide to Reading Strategies on pages xii–xiv.

Understanding Definitions

Choose the sentence that best reflects the meaning of the main sentence.
Look specifically at the underlined words or phrases. Explain your choice.

1. Coffee and cyberspace <u>collided</u> to form a new hybrid called the
   cybercafé.
   a. Coffee and cyberspace mixed together and became the cybercafé.
   b. Coffee and cyberspace clashed and the cybercafé resulted.

2. It was a <u>crude bastardization</u> of a <u>caffeinated icon</u> <u>heretofore</u> associated with Sartre.

   a. It was a rough version of the symbolic coffeehouse previously associated with Sartre.

   b. It was the rough coffeehouse symbol previously known as Sartre.

3. Revolution can be <u>debated with comrades</u> <u>sipping espresso</u> <u>thousands of miles away</u>.

   a. Revolution can be discussed with friends who are drinking espresso far away.

   b. Distant revolutions can be discussed with friends while drinking espresso.

4. <u>The digital elite</u> <u>have boycotted</u> <u>the digital coffeehouse</u>.

   a. Computer experts do not go to coffeehouses.

   b. Computer experts do not go to cybercafés.

5. Kit Galloway <u>derides</u> many of the newcomers as "<u>cybermats</u>."

   a. Kit Galloway doesn't like the new cybercafés.

   b. Kit Galloway goes to many of the new cybercafés.

6. Two young men were <u>entwined in the psychic combat</u> of the game Quake.

   a. Two young men were playing the computer game Quake.

   b. Two young men were arguing about the computer game Quake.

7. Yaakov said, "I'm trying to <u>set straight</u> the atheists and the evolutionists."

   a. Yaakov is trying to make friends with the atheists and evolutionists.

   b. Yaakov is trying to correct the atheists and evolutionists.

8. Colleen was <u>typing her response to an e-mail discussion</u> on jungle music vs. hip-hop <u>unfolding somewhere in the ether</u>.

   a. Colleen was responding to a discussion that took place in the café.

   b. Colleen was responding to a discussion on the Internet.

9. You don't have to <u>engage in some kind of bogus conversation</u> about yoga.

   a. You don't have to have a conversation about yoga, which is unnatural.

   b. You don't have to have an unnatural conversation about yoga.

10. Joy was <u>ensconced</u> with a friend on a low-slung couch drinking plain coffee.

   a. Joy was sitting comfortably with a friend on the couch and drinking coffee.

   b. Joy was arguing with a friend on the couch and drinking coffee.

VOCABULARY
**Creating
New Words**

Many new words are arising out of the technical revolution. Look at the following examples from the reading.

$cybercafé = cyber + café$

$cyberspace = cyber + space$

$cybermat = cyber + mat$ (from *laundromat*)

$caféculture = café + culture$

Here are some more word parts that are found frequently in discussing technology:

byte   *mega*   *net*   *web*   *digi* (or *digital*)

Give examples of new words using these parts:

_____ _____ _____ _____

Create three new words using the word parts above and using other common English words. Write definitions for them. Include an example sentence of how your "new" word is used.

1. Word: _____

Definition: _____

_____

Example Sentence: _____

2. Word: _____

Definition: _____

_____

Example Sentence: _____

3. Word: _____

Definition: _____

_____

Example Sentence: _____

Share your new words with your classmates.

THINK ABOUT IT

1. Would you visit a cybercafé? Why or why not?

2. What benefits do you think a cybercafé offers?

3. Why do you think coffeehouses, or cafés, have become popular in the United States?

Before You Read

"BEEN HERE LONG?"

Not everyone is happy with technological developments. The author of this reading explains why he believes that personal computers are not beneficial to society.

Before you read, think about these questions:

- Have you learned to use a computer? Why or why not?
- Do you fear computers? Why or why not?

About the Author

Wendell Berry was born in 1934 in rural Kentucky, where he also attended college. He is a farmer as well as a writer concerned with the environment, as this essay shows.

Why I Won't Buy a Computer

by Wendell Berry   Like almost everybody else, I am hooked to the energy corporations, which I do not admire. I hope to become less hooked to them. In my work, I try to be as little hooked to them as possible. As a farmer, I do almost all of my work with horses. As a writer, I work with a pencil or a pen and a piece

5   of paper.

My wife types my work on a Royal standard typewriter bought new in 1956 and as good now as it was then. As she types, she sees things that are wrong and marks them with small checks in the margins. She is my best critic because she is the one most familiar with my habitual errors and weaknesses. She also understands, sometimes better than I do, what *ought* to be said. We have, I think, a literary cottage industry that works well and pleasantly. I do not see anything wrong with it.

A number of people, by now, have told me that I would greatly improve things by buying a computer. My answer is that I am not going to do it. I have several reasons, and they are good ones.

The first is the one I mentioned in the beginning. I would hate to think that my work as a writer could not be done without direct dependence on strip-mined coal. How could I conscientiously write against the rape of nature if I were, in the act of writing, implicated in the rape? For the same reason, it matters to me that my writing is done in the daytime without electric light.

I do not admire the computer manufacturers a great deal more than I admire the energy industries. I have seen their advertisements, attempting to seduce struggling or failing farmers into the belief that they can solve their problems by buying yet another piece of expensive equipment. I do not see that computers are bringing us one step nearer to anything that does matter to me: peace, economic justice, ecological health, political honesty, family and community, stability, good work.

What would a computer cost me? More money, for one thing, than I can afford, and more than I wish to pay to people whom I do not admire. But the cost would not be just monetary. It is well understood that technological innovation always requires the discarding of the "old model"—the "old model" in this case being not just our old Royal standard, but my wife, my critic, my closest reader, my fellow worker. Thus (and I think this is typical of present-day technological innovation), what would be superseded would be not only something, but somebody. In order to be technologically up-to-date as a writer, I would have to sacrifice an association that I am dependent upon and that I treasure.

My final and perhaps my best reason for not owning a computer is that I do not wish to fool myself. I disbelieve, and therefore strongly resent, the assertion that I or anybody else could write better or more easily with a computer than with a pencil.

To make myself as plain as I can, I should give my standards for technological innovation in my own work. They are as follows:

1. The new tool should be cheaper than the one it replaces.

2. It should be at least as small in scale as the one it replaces.

3. It should do work that is clearly and demonstrably better than the one it replaces.

4. It should use less energy than the one it replaces.

50 **5.** If possible, it should use some form of solar energy, such as that of the body.

6. It should be repairable by a person of ordinary intelligence, provided that he or she has the necessary tools.

7. It should be purchasable and repairable as near to home as possible.

55 **8.** It should come from a small, privately owned shop or store that will take it back for maintenance and repair.

Source: From *Bread Loaf Quarterly/New England Review*

9. It should not replace or disrupt anything good that already exists, and this includes family and community relationships.

Check Your Comprehension

1. Why doesn't the author admire either the energy corporations or the computer manufacturers?

2. What does the author think a computer would "cost" him?

3. Given the author's "standards for technological innovation," what other new tools would he probably not want to buy?

READING

Find out more about **understanding arguments** by looking in the Reference Guide to Reading Strategies on pages xii–xiv.

Understanding Arguments

In this reading, the author is making an argument. Summarize the points of his argument below.

Why Wendell Berry won't buy a computer:

Reason 1: _____

Reason 2: _____

Reason 3: _____

Reason 4. _____

Do you agree with his argument? Why or why not?

VOCABULARY
Related Nouns and Verbs

Many nouns and verbs in English have identical forms. For example:

Many power companies *mine* coal. *(verb)*
They found the coal in a *mine. (noun)*

Others have different, yet related forms.

He *begins* each sentence with the word "but." *(verb)*
He starts at the *beginning. (noun)*

For each of the nouns or verbs in the table, write a related noun or verb. In some cases, there may not be a related word. If that is so, put an **X** in the space. The first one is done for you.

Verbs	**Nouns**
1. admire	admiration
2.	answer
3.	assertion
4. criticize	
5.	disbelief
6. discard	
7. disrupt	
8.	error
9	honesty
10. hook	
11.	mark
12.	model
13. own	
14. purchase	
15.	reason
16. require	
17. resent	
18.	sacrifice
19.	technology
20. write	

THINK ABOUT IT

1. One reason Berry says he doesn't want a computer is that his wife would no longer be included in his work. Do you think he is right? Why or why not?

2. Berry claims his reasons for not wanting a computer are "good ones." Do you agree? Which ones are good, and which are not, in your opinion?

3. Many people would disagree with Mr. Berry, saying that modern inventions are "labor-saving" devices. Without them, many argue, people are slaves to boring repetitive work. Do you agree? What do you think life was like before labor-saving inventions such as washing machines, vacuum cleaners, and dishwashers?

4. What is the relationship between the cartoon at the beginning of this reading and the reading?

5. Mr. Berry uses horses instead of farm machinery, and a typewriter instead of a computer. He also says he works during the day so that he does not have to use electric light. With a partner, list ten other modern inventions that are used in daily life. Then, using his nine rules for technological innovation, think of a substitute for that invention. List the replacement's advantages and disadvantages. The first one is done for you.

	Invention	Replacement	Advantages	Disadvantages
1.	telephone	writing letters	letters cost less	letters aren't useful in emergencies; they're too slow
2.				
3.				
4.				
5.				
6.				
7.				
8.				
9.				
10.				

PART TWO

Information: **The More You Know**

Many people complain that there is too much information now.
Dozens of television channels, newspapers, and the Internet all contribute to
a glut of information. How does this much information affect a culture?
This section looks at this question.

Before You Read

Cellular Phone Service Statistics, 1985-1997

Number of cellular phone service subscribers, 1985: 203,600

Number of cellular phone service subscribers, 1997: 48,700,000

Cellular service revenues, 1985: $354,000,000

Cellular service revenues, 1997: $25,600,000,000

Cellular service sites, 1985: 599

Cellular service sites, 1997: 38,000

Average monthly cellular service bill, 1988: $95

Average monthly cellular service bill, 1997: $43

Source: Communicating
Online
http://www.commnews.com/

In the following essay, the author talks about the unusual combination of
the wilderness and technology.

Before you read this article, think about the following questions:

- Do you have a cellular telephone? If you do, do you take it
  everywhere?

- If you don't have a cellular telephone, would you like to have one?
  Why or why not?

- Do you like to go camping?

Cultural Cues

Swiss Army knife A popular pocket knife, usually red, with a Swiss emblem on it.

Coast Guard A government agency responsible for patrolling and guarding America's waters.

Mt. Rainier A large mountain in the Cascade mountain range in Washington state.

Vineyard Sound A body of water near Martha's Vineyard, an island south of Boston, off the coast of Massachusetts.

Cell Phones in the Wilderness

by R. H. Wheatley
Try bringing a Swiss Army knife instead.

Camping areas in New Hampshire's White Mountains are abuzz these days with cellular phones as well-heeled backpackers phone their brokers. Boaters on Vineyard Sound consult their pocket Global Positioning Systems
5   (GPS) and announce proudly, "Well, Martha, we are right here in the harbor!"

A quick scan through a popular magazine for those who fancy themselves outdoor types reveals more ads for electronics than for sleeping bags or hiking boots. The boating magazines are even worse, filled with gadgetry guaranteed to eliminate any need for you to learn what a chart is. Everything
10   short of pocket fax machines, and no doubt they will be featured at next year's backpacking exposition.

The Coast Guard, established to rescue mariners and fishermen who faced the wrath of the sea, now spends a great deal of time responding to weekend boaters who didn't think to bring a compass but made sure to
15   pack the cellular telephone so they could dial 911 when the ice in the cooler ran low.

The Forest Service in New Hampshire reports that this past summer a businessman called from the crest of the Presidential Range and demanded a helicopter ride out because he was going to be late for a business appointment.
20   A couple years ago, a party of hikers on Mt. Rainier in April were caught by a snow storm and credited their cell phone with saving their lives. They had only summer clothes and no sleeping bags.

A GPS which pinpoints the location of your boat to a quarter of a mile is a waste if you don't know how to cope with the currents or the fog, or
25   if you don't know where the rocks are. Or if you forgot to fuel up before you left.

Nature hasn't changed. It still punishes the stupid and the unprepared. Bluntly put, there are a lot more idiots going to the woods and the mountains and out to sea these days. These intrepid outdoorspeople apparently feel
30   safer with their expensive electronics. But this is a dangerous illusion. The gadgets don't keep them out of trouble. They just make it possible for them to call for help when they find themselves inconvenienced or in danger, incurring public expense, using up scarce emergency resources, and in some cases jeopardizing the safety of other people.
35   The outdoors has not gotten any safer, just more accessible for the totally unprepared.

Source: "What I Think"

Check Your Comprehension

1. What is GPS? What does it do?

2. What cell phone related problems does the Coast Guard face?

3. According to the author, do cell phones make going into the wilderness safer? Why or why not?

READING

Find out more about **understanding point of view** by looking in the Reference Guide to Reading Strategies on pages xii–xiv.

Understanding Point of View

What is the author's attitude towards electronic gadgets and the people who use them in the wilderness?

In order to answer this question, look for specific sentences in the reading that show this attitude. List six of those sentences here. The first one is done for you. Explain what each sentence means.

Sentence	Explanation
1. Try bringing a Swiss Army knife instead.	A practical tool, like a knife, is more useful than a cellular phone.
2.	
3.	
4.	
5.	
6.	

VOCABULARY
Using New Vocabulary

This reading presents several words that might be new to you. Show that you understand these words by completing the sentences below.

1. The room was **abuzz** when ⎯⎯⎯⎯⎯⎯⎯⎯⎯⎯⎯⎯⎯⎯ .

2. You use a **compass** to ⎯⎯⎯⎯⎯⎯⎯⎯⎯⎯⎯⎯⎯⎯ .

3. He **fancies himself** ⎯⎯⎯⎯⎯⎯⎯⎯⎯⎯⎯⎯⎯⎯ .

4. He was an **intrepid** hiker; he ⎯⎯⎯⎯⎯⎯⎯⎯⎯⎯⎯⎯ .

5. My cousin is very **well-heeled;** she ⎯⎯⎯⎯⎯⎯⎯⎯⎯⎯ .

6. He showed his **wrath** when he ⎯⎯⎯⎯⎯⎯⎯⎯⎯⎯⎯ .

THINK ABOUT IT

CNN VIDEO Watch the CNN video on cell phones.

Discuss these questions:

1. Who uses cell phones most?

2. According to the report, why do people use cell phones?

1. Do you agree with the author's attitude towards cell phones? Why or why not?

2. What new technological gadgets do you own, or would you like to own?

3. Look at a magazine for advertisements for new gadgets—such as the "pocket fax" mentioned by the author. Bring your advertisements to class and explain the gadgets to your classmates.

4. Think about an invention that would make your life easier. Write a short description of what this gadget would do, and how you would use it. Share your ideas with your classmates.

Good Afternoon

Welcome to the
White House

The President & Vice President:
Their accomplishments, their families, and how to send them electronic mail --

Commonly Requested Federal Services:
Direct access to Federal Services

Interactive Citizens' Handbook: Your guide to information about the Federal government

What's New:
What's happening at the White House -
President Clinton Delivers Commencement Address to MIT Graduates

White House History and Tours:
Past Presidents and First Families, Art in the President's House and Tours -- **Tour Information**

Site News:
Recent additions to our site -
-Vice President's Welfare-to-Work Coalition
-President's Initiative on Race

-White House Millennium Council

The Virtual Library:
Search White House documents, listen to speeches, and view photos

The Briefing Room:
Today's releases, hot topics, and the latest Federal statistics

White House Help Desk:
Frequently asked questions and answers about our service

White House for Kids:
Helping young people become more active and informed citizens

In this reading, the President and Vice President of the United States make an important announcement.

Before you read, think about the following questions:

- Have you ever sent an e-mail message to a politician or other famous person?
- Do you think e-mail is improving democracy?

Cultural Cues   *Congress* The U.S. Congress, or legislative part of the U.S. government, consisting of the House of Representatives and the Senate

Letter from the President and Vice President in Announcement of White House Electronic Mail Address

June 1, 1993

Dear Friends:

Part of our commitment to change is to keep the White House in step with today's changing technology. As we move ahead into the 21st century,
5 we must have a government that can show the way and lead by example. Today, we are pleased to announce that for the first time in history, the White House will be connected to you via electronic mail. Electronic mail will bring the Presidency and this Administration closer and make it more accessible to the people.
10   The White House will be connected to the Internet as well as several on-line commercial vendors, thus making us more accessible and more in touch with people across this country. We will not be alone in this venture. Congress is also getting involved, and an exciting announcement regarding electronic mail is expected to come from the House of Representatives
15 tomorrow.
    Various government agencies also will be taking part in the near future. Americans Communicating Electronically is a project developed by several government agencies to coordinate and improve access to the nation's educational and information assets and resources. This will be done through
20 interactive communications such as electronic mail, and brought to people who do not have ready access to a computer.
    However, we must be realistic about the limitations and expectations of the White House electronic mail system. This experiment is the first-ever e-mail project done on such a large scale. As we work to reinvent government
25 and streamline our processes, the e-mail project can help to put us on the leading edge of progress.

Initially, your e-mail message will be read and receipt immediately acknowledged. A careful count will be taken on the number received as well as the subject of each message. However, the White House is not yet capable
30 of sending back a tailored response via electronic mail. We are hoping this will happen by the end of the year.

A number of response-based programs which allow technology to help us read your message more effectively, and, eventually respond to you electronically in a timely fashion will be tried out as well. These programs
35 will change periodically as we experiment with the best way to handle electronic mail from the public. Since this has never been tried before, it is important to allow for some flexibility in the system in these first stages. We welcome your suggestions.

This is an historic moment in the White House and we look forward to
40 your participation and enthusiasm for this milestone event. We eagerly anticipate the day when electronic mail from the public is an integral and normal part of the White House communications system.

President Clinton   *Vice President Gore*

Check Your Comprehension

1. What is the purpose of the letter from the White House?

2. What is "Americans Communicating Electronically"?

3. What is the process of reading and responding to e-mail at the White House?

READING

Find out more about **summarizing** by looking in the Reference Guide to Reading Strategies on pages xii–xiv.

Summarizing

Summarize this announcement using the box below. Compare your summary with a classmate's. Which things did you leave out, and which did you include? After reading your classmate's summary, would you change your summary? How?

_____

_____

_____

_____

_____

_____

_____

_____

VOCABULARY
Prepositions

This reading contains several phrases that use prepositions in ways that might be new to you. Fill in the correct preposition in each blank; then, write a sentence using the phrase shown. You may change the verb tenses.

1. to lead _____ example

   _____

   _____

2. to keep _____ step _____ technology

   _____

   _____

3. the first time _____ history

   _____

   _____

4. to be _____ touch _____ the people

   _____

   _____

5. to be alone _____ this venture

   _____

   _____

6. to take part _____ the experiment

   _____

   _____

7. to do something _____ a large scale

   _____

   _____

THINK ABOUT IT

1. If you have access to the World Wide Web, look at the White House site (http://www.whitehouse.gov) and report on it to your class. What things did you find there?

2. What is your opinion of the process by which the White House responds to the e-mail it receives? Why do you think it is structured as it is?

3. If you use e-mail, write a message to the White House about a topic that concerns you. Report back to your class about the response you receive.

SYNTHESIS

Discussion and Debate

1. Much criticism of new technology seems to come from older generations. Why do you think this is the case? Why do you think younger people seem to adapt more easily to new technologies?

2. How does the use of technology in the United States compare to that in your country? Do Americans use more or less technology? In what ways is it used differently?

3. Should the Internet be censored? What should be censored and for what reasons? Organize a debate in your class in which you argue for one side of this issue.

4. Think of another question to ask your classmates about the ideas presented in this chapter.

Writing Topics

1. How has the computer affected daily life? Write a short essay in which you illustrate what your day would be like if computers did not exist.

2. What new words has the age of technology introduced into English? Reread the articles in this chapter, look at the technology section of the newspaper, survey computer magazines, or whatever other materials are available to you, to find technology-related words that you think are new to English. Create a glossary of new words. It may help to do this with a partner or small group.

3. Choose one of the items below, and write an essay explaining how this item has changed human communication:

   fax machine   cellular telephone   e-mail
   Internet   telephone   television

On Your Own

1. The following films have technology as a theme. Rent one from a video store or check it out of the library and watch it

   The Net   *2001: A Space Odyssey*   *Johnny Mnemonic*
   1984   *Sneakers*   *Brave New World*

2. Go to a computer store and gather information about different personal computers. Collect any brochures and price lists they have. Choose which new computer you would like to buy, based on the information you gather.

3. Look at a current issue of a computer magazine. Find an article in it that interests you. Report on the article to your classmates.

★★

A L M A N A C   For additional cultural information, refer to the Almanac on pages 221–234. The Almanac contains lists of useful facts, maps, and other information to enhance your learning.

★★★

Popular Culture

American popular culture embraces all forms of
entertainment as well as sports, fashion, and cultural icons.
This chapter looks at some of these areas of
American "pop" culture.

PART ONE

All Decked Out

Is there an "American style" of clothing?
The next two readings consider that idea.

Before You Read

Levi's Pants

The flashes of violence and miracles do not blind Levi Strauss, who arrives from far-off Bavaria and realizes at one blink that here the beggar becomes a millionaire and the millionaire a beggar or corpse in a click of cards or triggers. In another blink he discovers that pants become tatters in these mines of California, and decides to provide a better fate for the strong cloths he has brought along. He won't sell awnings or tents. He will sell pants, tough pants for tough men in the tough work of digging up rivers and mines. So the seams won't burst, he reinforces them with copper riveting. Behind, under the waist, Levi stamps his name on a leather label.

Soon the cowboys of the whole West will claim as their own these pants of blue Nîmes twill which neither sun nor years wear out.

Source: *Memory of Fire: Faces and Masks*, Eduardo Galeano, Random House, Inc.

This reading concerns the history of blue jeans and how this simple, working-class piece of clothing has influenced fashion in the United States and throughout the world.

Before you read, think about the following questions:

- Do you own blue jeans? When do you wear them?
- Why do you think jeans have become so popular?

Cultural Cues

James Dean, John Wayne, Marlon Brando Three movie stars who were popular in the middle part of the twentieth century; they were popular for their "tough guy" images.

Jimmy Carter The 39th president of the United States.

Benelux nations Belgium, the Netherlands, and Luxembourg.

North Bronx A middle-class neighborhood in New York City

Williams College A college in Williamstown, Massachusetts.

About the Author

John Brooks is a writer who has worked as a contributing editor to *Time* magazine. He has also written novels and books on the history of American business.

Dressing Down

by John Brooks Beyond doubt, the jeans phenomenon is a seismic event in the history of dress, and not only in the United States. Indeed, the habit of wearing jeans is—along with the computer, the copying machine, rock music, polio vaccine, and the hydrogen bomb—one of the major contributions of the United
5 States to the postwar world at large.

Before the nineteen-fifties, jeans were worn, principally in the West and Southwest of the United States, by children, farmers, manual laborers when on the job, and, of course, cowboys. There were isolated exceptions—for example, artists of both sexes took to blue jeans in and around Santa Fe,
10 New Mexico, in the nineteen-twenties and -thirties; around 1940, the male students at Williams College took them up as a mark of differentiation from the chino-wearing snobs of Yale and Princeton; and in the late forties the female students of Bennington College (not far from Williams) adopted them as a virtual uniform, though only for wear on campus—but it was not until
15 the nineteen-fifties, when James Dean and Marlon Brando wore jeans in movies about youth in revolt against parents and society, when John Wayne wore them in movies about untrammeled heroes in a lawless Old West, and when many schools from coast to coast gave their new symbolism a boost by banning them as inappropriate for classrooms, that jeans acquired the
20 ideological baggage necessary to propel them to national fame.

After that, though, fame came quickly, and it was not long before young Americans—whether to express social dissent, to enjoy comfort, or to emu-

late their peers—had become so attached to their jeans that some hardly ever took them off. According to a jeans authority, a young man in the North
25 Bronx with a large and indulgent family attained some sort of record by continuously wearing the same pair of jeans, even for bathing and sleeping, for over eight months. Eventually, as all the world knows, the popularity of jeans spread from cowboys and anomic youths to adult Americans of virtually every age and sociopolitical posture, conspicuously including Jimmy
30 Carter when he was a candidate for the presidency. Trucks containing jeans came to rank as one of the three leading targets of hijackers, along with those containing liquor and cigarettes. Estimates of jeans sales in the United States vary wildly, chiefly because the line between jeans and slacks has come to be a fuzzy one. According to the most conservative figures, put
35 out by the leading jeans manufacturer, Levi Strauss & Company, of San Francisco, annual sales of jeans of all kinds in the United States by all manufacturers in 1957 stood at around a hundred and fifty million pairs, while for 1977 they came to over five hundred million, or considerably more than two pairs for every man, woman, and child in the country.
40   Overseas, jeans had to wait slightly longer for their time to come. American Western movies and the example of American servicemen from the West and Southwest stationed abroad who, as soon as the Second World War ended, changed directly from their service uniforms into blue jeans bought at post exchanges started a fad for them among Europeans in the
45 late nineteen-forties. But the fad remained a small one, partly because of the unavailability of jeans in any quantity; in those days, European customers considered jeans ersatz unless they came from the United States, while United States jeans manufacturers were inclined to be satisfied with a reliable domestic market. Being perennially short of denim, the rough, dura-
50 ble, naturally shrink-and stretch cotton twill of which basic jeans are made, they were reluctant or unable to undertake overseas expansion.
        Gradually, though, denim production in the United States increased, and meanwhile demand for American-made jeans became so overwhelming that in parts of Europe a black market for them developed. American jeans
55 manufacturers began exporting their product in a serious way in the early nineteen-sixties. At first, the demand was greatest in Germany, France, England, and the Benelux nations; later it spread to Italy, Spain, and Scandinavia, and eventually to Latin America and the Far East. By 1967, jeans authorities estimate, a hundred and ninety million pairs of jeans were being
60 sold annually outside the United States; of these, all but a small fraction were of local manufacture, and not imports from the United States, although American-made jeans were still so avidly sought after that some of the local products were blatant counterfeits of the leading American brands, complete with expertly faked labels. In the late nineteen-seventies, estimated jeans
65 sales outside the United States had doubled in a decade, to three hundred and eighty million pairs, of which perhaps a quarter were now made by American firms in plants abroad; the markets in Europe, Mexico, Japan, Australia, and other places had come so close to the saturation point that

the fastest-growing jeans market was probably Brazil; Princess Anne of
70 Great Britain, and Princess Caroline of Monaco, had been photographed
wearing jeans, and King Hussein of Jordan was reported to wear them at
home in his palace; the counterfeiting of American brands was a huge
international undertaking, which the leading American manufacturers com-
bated with world-ranging security operations. In Russia, authentic American
75 Levis were a black-market item regularly commanding eighty or more dollars
per pair. All in all, it is now beyond doubt that in size and scope the rapid
global spread of the habit of wearing blue jeans, however it may be explained,
is an event without precedent in the history of human attire.

Source: *Showing Off in
America*

Check Your Comprehension

1. According to the author, what events caused jeans to become nationally popular?

2. What are some of the signs that indicate the popularity of jeans?

3. Why were European countries so slow in adopting jeans as a popular style?

READING

Find out more about **scanning** by looking in the Reference Guide to Reading Strategies on pages xii–xiv.

Scanning

This reading presents a history of blue jeans. Scan the article quickly and fill out the information below.

1. Who (primarily) wore jeans in the following time periods?

   1920s and 1930s _____

   1940s _____

   1950s _____

2. What was the annual U.S. sales of blue jeans in these years:

   1957 _____

   1977 _____

3. What were the sales figures for jeans sold outside the U.S.?

   Sales by 1967 _____

   Sales by the late 1970s _____

VOCABULARY
Vocabulary in Context

Rewrite each sentence, paraphrasing the italicized word or phrase.

1. The jeans phenomenon is a *seismic event* in the history of dress.

_____

2. John Wayne wore jeans in movies about *untrammeled* heroes in the lawless Old West.

_____

3. Jeans acquired the *ideological* baggage necessary to propel them to national fame.

_____

4. The popularity of jeans spread from cowboys and *anomic youths* to adult Americans.

_____

5. European customers considered jeans *ersatz* unless they came from the United States.

_____

6. Some of the local products were *blatant counterfeits* of the leading American brands.

_____

THINK ABOUT IT

1. Four recent U.S. presidents—Jimmy Carter, Ronald Reagan, George Bush, and Bill Clinton—have been known to wear jeans publicly. Can you think of any other world leaders who wear blue jeans? What do you think it says about American politicians in general?

2. Although blue jeans have been a popular fashion for decades, the style in which blue jeans are worn changes. For example, in the 1960s, baggy Levis were popular, in the 1970s, tighter designer jeans were the fashion. What is the current style of blue jeans?

3. How have blue jeans been accepted into your culture? Who wears them? What places do they wear them to? How much do they cost compared to other pants?

4. Look through magazines or newspapers for advertisements for blue jeans. Try to find ads for different brands. How do the ads differ? What type would you like to buy, on the basis of the advertising? Bring your ads to class for discussion.

Before You Read

In this reading, the author, a cartoonist, makes fun of the dress that is required in the American office. This reading contains both a short essay and some cartoons by the author on the subject of business clothing.

Before you read, think about the following questions:

- What is "standard" business attire like in your country?
- How is business dress different from everyday clothing?
- Why do you think businesses adopt certain dress codes?

Cultural Cues

HR Human Resources, a department of a company, sometimes referred to as the Personnel Department.

Casual (or Dress-Down) Fridays A recent business practice, in which employees are allowed to dress less formally on Fridays.

About the Author

Scott Adams received his Masters of Business Administration (M.B.A.) from the University of California, Berkeley. He worked in business for nine years before starting his popular comic strip, *Dilbert.* He lives in the San Francisco Bay area.

Dress Clothes

by Scott Adams

Nothing is more adorable than one of those little organ-grinder monkeys with a tiny vest and a hat. That would be the official uniform at your company too if not for the fact it would be considered a "uniform" and there's no budget for that sort of thing.

Companies have long discovered a low-cost method for making people dress in the same humiliating fashion as the monkey but without the expense of buying uniforms. The secret is to specify a style of acceptable dress that has the same symbolism as the monkey's outfit but allows some variety:

Clothing	Symbolism
Necktie	Leash
Pantyhose	Leg irons; prisoner
Suit jacket	Penguin; incapable of flight
High heels	Masochism

Check Your Comprehension

1. Why does the author think there are no uniforms at most companies?

2. What is the author's opinion of work dress codes?

3. In the comic strip, why does "Catbert" not allow jeans to be worn on Casual Fridays?

4. What is funny about the "new casual dress code" in the last comic strip?

READING

Find out more about **understanding humor** by looking in the Reference Guide to Reading Strategies on pages xii–xiv.

Understanding Humor

This reading is intended to be humorous—however, humor is sometimes the most difficult thing to explain or understand in a second language.

Identify passages in the reading and in the comics that are intended to be humorous. Then, explain what makes these passages humorous. For example:

1. Comparing business dress to a monkey's costume

   This might be funny because many people find monkeys humorous.

2. _____

3. _____

4. _____

Did you find these things funny? Why or why not?

VOCABULARY
Paraphrasing

Here are two sentences from the reading. Paraphrase them, using words or sentence structures that are more familiar to you.

1. So, casual clothes *don't* lower our stock value, but only if worn on Fridays, unless somebody sees us.

   _____

   _____

2. I love the "Business Casual" look for the way it combines unattractive with unprofessional while diminishing neither.

   _____

   _____

THINK ABOUT IT

1. Many professions require uniforms. Think about each profession below, and explain why it might require a uniform.

   police officer   basketball player
   soldier   waiter (in some restaurants)

2. Did you wear a uniform to school when you were a child? If so, did you like it? If not, would you have liked to wear one? What is your opinion of school uniforms?

3. There is an English saying, "Clothes make the man." What does this mean? Do you agree?

PART TWO

Icons: Larger Than Life

Icons are symbols that stand for complex ideas, religious beliefs, or even entire cultures. In this part of the chapter, two American icons, Elvis Presley and Superman, are examined.

Before You Read

Do You Want to Visit Graceland?

Graceland: Reservations are recommended. The mansion tour is $10 for adults, $9 for senior citizens, $5 for ages 7–12. The platinum tour—which includes Elvis' airplanes, the car collection and the Sincerely Elvis museum—is $18.50 for adults, $16.65 for seniors, $11 for ages 7–12. Hours are 8 a.m.–6 p.m., seven days, 800-238-2000.

Lodging: A handful of hotel rooms ($130 range) are available. Memphis Convention and Visitors Bureau, 800-873-6282; Visitors Information Center, 901-543-5333.

Dining: Elvis Presley's Memphis, a Beale Street theme restaurant devoted to the King, features Elvis favorites such as the peanut butter and fried banana sandwich ($4.75) and meatloaf ($6.25). 11 a.m.–midnight Sunday–Thursday, until 3 a.m. Friday and Saturday, 901-527-6900.

**READING**

Find out more about **skimming** by looking in the Reference Guide to Reading Strategies on pages xii–xiv.

Skimming

Skimming means reading quickly to get the main ideas. Read this article quickly. Take only two minutes. Then write down three main ideas that you understand from the reading.

1. _____

_____

2. _____

_____

3. _____

_____

 Watch the CNN video on the Elvis conference.

Discuss these questions:

1. What events occur at the Elvis conference?

2. Who attends the conference?

3. What is the purpose of the conference?

In this reading, the author discusses the enormous popularity of Elvis Presley, decades after his death.

Before you read, think about these questions:

- Have you ever heard Elvis Presley's music? Did you like it?
- Have you seen any Elvis movies?
- Is Elvis popular in your country?

Still the King
Interest Shows No Sign of Waning
by Clifford Rothman

Memphis—The First Presleyterian Church of Elvis the Divine.

It's no joke. Organized worship is one of countless offshoots of Elvis Presley's mush-
5 rooming legacy.

As Memphis, and up to 100,000 visiting fans, prepare for the 20th anniversary of his death on August 16, Elvis has moved beyond legend and almost past myth.

10 More than 500 active fan clubs and a handful of Elvis churches revere him. His record sales, already exceeding a billion, grow as new global markets and new generations discover the King of rock 'n' roll. Academics study him.
15 About 750,000 fans tour Graceland, his Memphis home and the cornerstone of the Elvis industry, each year.

But will it last?

When nobody from Elvis' lifetime is around to remember, will crowds still flock to Graceland, listen to his records, worship his image?

Or will he wane, like every famous performer and all but a few historical figures, taking with him a reported $75 million-a-year business driven by image licensing and Graceland-related tourism?

"Elvis changed U.S. culture in profound and unprecedented ways, more than any other 20th century figure," says Gilbert Rodman of the University of South Florida, author of *Elvis After Elvis: The Posthumous Career of a Living Legend* and part of a burgeoning group of Elvis scholars.

"Classic theories of stardom and the media suggest that once a star is dead and no longer producing a new product, their presence will fade," he says. "What's happening with Elvis is the opposite. Elvis is harder to avoid today, even if you don't like him, than he was 20 years ago. And that's not showing any signs of stopping any time soon."

"There is no popular cultural figure, whether it's John Lennon or Frank Sinatra, who has equivalent power to generate interest throughout the world," adds Bill Ferris, director of the Center for the Study of Southern Culture at the University of Mississippi.

Already, academics study Elvis as a role model for the first stages of a new religion. Some suggest parallels between Elvis' following and the early stages of major religions.

"We seem to be at that point where you can intelligently talk about an emerging quasi-religious movement," says comparative religions professor Norman Girardot, who teaches a course on Elvis at Lehigh University in Bethlehem, Pa.

"There are parallels in the origins of Christianity, Buddhism, Confucianism and the Elvis movement."

And the market for that movement is spreading. More than half of Graceland's visitors were born after Presley's death. His records sell strongly in Russia and China. A dozen Elvis restaurants are projected throughout the USA and overseas in the next decade.

"The universe is expanding far beyond those who witnessed him on stage and spent their adolescence listening to Elvis songs," says Vernon Chadwick, founder of the International Conference on Elvis (August 10–15 in Memphis), which examines the growing significance of Elvis.

"Like any other myth or religion, it will take on a life of its own after the historical players have left the building."

Both Memphis and Elvis Presley Enterprises, the 550-employee behemoth led by the singer's ex-wife Priscilla, are working to ensure the viability of the Presley name.

The two are discussing the transformation of Elvis Presley Boulevard, a commercialized thoroughfare approaching Graceland, into a scenic parkway with a grassy median and an arched gateway.

"It would create an atmosphere that would justly celebrate Elvis," says Kevin Kane of the Memphis Convention and Visitors Bureau.

EPE [Elvis Presley Enterprises], which keeps the grounds of Graceland as unchanged as possible, plans a large exhibition center nearby to tell the Elvis story and showcase a trove of warehoused artifacts.

"Unlike the 380 visitors to Graceland per hour, a well laid-out exhibition hall could handle 800 to 1,000 per hour or higher," says Jack Soden, CEO of EPE. "It will go to the design stage in six months, with a development period of two years."

Graceland itself, built in 1939 as a family residence for a prominent Memphis doctor, can easily withstand the rigors of the 50 million visitors projected over the next 50 years.

"The house is absolutely enduring, built of the finest materials at the time," says William Eubanks, the Memphis- and Manhattan-based interior designer who decorated the TV and pool rooms at Graceland.

When Elvis died in 1977, the mansion was

deemed a white elephant. In 1982, Priscilla Presley invested the estate's remaining cash in tweaking Graceland from a private home into a public tour.

115 Since Graceland's opening, Priscilla has shown a Midas touch, buying adjacent property, opening seven related gift shops and three museums, and, most recently, launching a $4 million theme restaurant and nightclub on
120 Beale Street celebrating Elvis and his musical roots.

In its first two weeks, Elvis Presley's Memphis has opened every day to waiting lines.

"We're doing 4,000 to 5,000 transactions a
125 day, and already sold out of three months worth of Elvis merchandise," says Michael Graves, operational manager of the project.

The Memphis-based restaurant will expand slowly in domestic and international sites, in-
130 cluding a Las Vegas hotel and casino.

Presley is still RCA's No. 1-selling artist, and the label has enough unreleased recordings to generate years' worth of new discs.

"We will be able to locate other material
135 we have the rights to that will result in very compelling Elvis Presley releases," says Michael Omansky, an RCA vice president. "I'd say (enough for) a minimum of five years, and very possibly at least another decade. And 10 years
140 is a lifetime in this business."

But will Presley's appeal be as potent in, say, 2047?

Experts offer a cautious yes. "What happens in the next 50 years will probably be as
145 unpredictable as it has in the past 20," Rodman says.

Ferris sees the Presley legacy strongly attracting future generations. "I project a steady growth of relationships between people in the
150 21st century and the life and persona of Elvis Presley," he says.

"There is a wondrous thing that happens when you hire or invite people into this Elvis world," says Priscilla Presley. "They literally
155 love it with a passion. They emulate him. If you are not an Elvis lover when you come into our organization, you leave an Elvis lover. It's quite a phenomenon."

If interest were to subside, would
160 Graceland revert to a private residence or be given to the National Park Service?

"We're not going to deal in exit strategies. Interest in this is so strong," Soden says. "And operating Graceland won't become a financial
165 burden any time soon. We hopefully will have managed and diversified for (Elvis' daughter) Lisa Marie's children and grandchildren."

But Memphis and Tennessee would readily snap up the home, which is listed on the Na-
170 tional Register of Historic Places.

"If the estate no longer wanted to maintain it, the city of Memphis or the state of Tennessee would definitely be interested," says Lois Riggins-Ezzell, executive director of the Tennessee
175 State Museum, which oversees historic property. "The fact is that Elvis is now a historical character. And Graceland is a national treasure and a state treasure. In fact, it is a part of world culture, and to not maintain it would be
180 a shame."

Others are glad that the city, which for years dismissed Elvis, has woken up to his worth.

"Memphis is finally coming around that this man is the thing that put Memphis on the map,
185 and keeps people coming to town," says Tim Sampson of *Memphis* magazine. "They're finally embracing the fact that Elvis is one of the greatest phenomena of the century.

"I also expected it to taper off 10 years ago.
190 And it just gets bigger and bigger and bigger."

Source: *USA Today*

Check Your Comprehension

1. What does the author mean by saying that organized worship is one of the offshoots of Elvis Presley's legacy?

2. What is Graceland?

3. What are the "classic theories of stardom of media"? How does Elvis defy these theories?

4. What new Elvis business ventures will be undertaken in the future?

VOCABULARY New Words

The following words and phrases are found in the reading. Show you understand their meanings by completing the sentences below.

1. One **offshoot** of Elvis's popularity is _____

_____ .

2. _____ is the **cornerstone** of the Elvis industry.

3. Elvis's popularity is burgeoning; in other words, it is _____

_____ .

4. A **behemoth** is _____ .

5. My room is a **trove** of _____ .

6. I cannot withstand the **rigors** of _____ .

7. _____ is a **white elephant.**

It _____ .

8. He has the **Midas touch;** everything he does _____

_____ .

9. When you **snap** something **up,** you

_____ .

10. When something **tapers off,** it _____

_____ .

THINK ABOUT IT

1. The reading says that there are parallels between Elvis-worship and religious development. What evidence is found in the article to support this idea? Do you agree?

2. The phrase "cultural icon" is used to explain things or people that symbolize an important aspect of culture. Marilyn Monroe, John F.

Kennedy, Elvis Presley, and Madonna are all considered cultural icons. Why do you think Elvis is such an important cultural icon?

3. If you have access to the Internet, search for web sites that feature Elvis Presley. How many did you find? Look for Frank Sinatra and John Lennon. Compare your findings. Do your findings support or go against the claim in the article that Elvis is much more important than either Sinatra or Lennon?

Before You Read

Boy reading Superman comic book

In the following article, the author discusses Superman, and why he is "typically American."

Before you read, think about the following questions:

- Have you seen the Superman television show or movies? If so, did you enjoy them?
- What other American superheroes are you familiar with?
- Who are the superheroes of your culture?

Cultural Cues

Davy Crockett An American figure, known as a frontiersman; Crockett fought and was killed at the battle of the Alamo, in San Antonio, Texas.

Paul Bunyan A mythical American figure who is known for clearing forests with the help of Babe, the Blue Ox.

Batman A comic book superhero who dresses like a bat.

Mike Fink A legendary character who explored the frontier by boat.

Pecos Bill A mythical cowboy character of Texas.

The Mayflower One of the ships that brought the earliest European settlers to America.

underground railroads Systems that helped slaves to escape from their owners in the South; these were not real railroads, but organizations of people that hid slaves and helped them move from place to place until they reached the free North.

About the Author

Gary Engle is an associate professor of English at Cleveland State University in Ohio. He has written over two hundred magazine and journal articles. He is also the author of a book called *The Grotesque Essence: Plays from American Minstrel Style.*

WHAT MAKES
Superman
SO DARNED AMERICAN ?

by Gary Engle   Superman is the great American hero. We are a nation rich with legendary figures. But among the Davy Crocketts and Paul Bunyans and Mike Finks and Pecos Bills and all the rest who speak for various regional identities in the pantheon of American folklore, only Superman achieves truly mythic
5   stature, interweaving a pattern of beliefs, literary conventions, and cultural traditions of the American people more powerfully and more accessibly than any other cultural symbol of the twentieth century, perhaps of any period in our history.

The core of the American myth in Superman consists of a few basic
10   facts that remain unchanged throughout the infinitely varied ways in which the myth is told—facts with which everyone is familiar, however marginal their knowledge of the story. Superman is an orphan rocketed to Earth when his native planet Krypton explodes; he lands near Smallville and is adopted by Jonathan and Martha Kent, who inculcate in him their American
15   middle-class ethic; as an adult he migrates to Metropolis where he defends

America—no, the world! no, the Universe!—from all evil and harm while playing a romantic game in which, as Clark Kent, he hopelessly pursues Lois Lane, who hopelessly pursues Superman, who remains aloof until such time as Lois proves worthy of him by falling in love with his feigned identity
20 as a weakling. That's it. Every narrative thread in the mythology, each one of the thousands of plots in the fifty-year stream of comics and films and TV shows, all the tales involving the demigods of the Superman pantheon—Superboy, Supergirl, even Krypto the Superdog—every single one reinforces by never contradicting this basic set of facts. That's the myth, and that's
25 where one looks to understand America.

It is impossible to imagine Superman being as popular as he is and speaking as deeply to the American character were he not an immigrant and an orphan. Immigration, of course, is the overwhelming fact in American history. Except for the Indians, all Americans have an immediate sense of
30 their origins elsewhere. No nation on Earth has so deeply embedded in its social consciousness the imagery of passage from one social identity to another: the Mayflower of the New England separatists, the slave ships from Africa and the subsequent underground railroads toward freedom in the North, the sailing ships and steamers running shuttles across two oceans
35 in the nineteenth century, the freedom airlifts in the twentieth. Somehow the picture just isn't complete without Superman's rocketship.

Like the peoples of the nation whose values he defends, Superman is an alien, but not just any alien. He's the consummate and totally uncompromised alien, an immigrant whose visible difference from the norm is underscored
40 by his decision to wear a costume of bold primary colors so tight as to be his very skin. Moreover, Superman the alien is real. He stands out among the hosts of comic book characters (Batman is a good example) for whom the superhero role is like a mask assumed when needed, a costume worn over their real identities as normal Americans. Superman's powers—
45 strength, mobility, x-ray vision and the like—are the comic-book equivalents of ethnic characteristics, and they protect and preserve the vitality of the foster community in which he lives in the same way that immigrant ethnicity has sustained American culture linguistically, artistically, economically, politically, and spiritually. The myth of Superman asserts with total confidence
50 and a childlike innocence the value of the immigrant in American culture.

Source: Excerpted from "What Makes Superman So Darned American?" *Superman at Fifty!*

Check Your Comprehension

1. How does Superman's mode of arriving on earth compare to the way other U.S. immigrants arrive?

2. According to the author, what is the similarity between Batman and Superman?

3. What is the meaning of Superman's bright clothing?

4. How does the author compare Superman's powers with the immigrant community?

READING

Find out more about **understanding arguments** by looking in the Reference Guide to Reading Strategies on pages xii–xiv.

Understanding Arguments

Restate the author's argument in one sentence. Then, state the reasons he gives in support of his argument.

Main argument: _____

_____

Reason 1. _____

_____

Reason 2. _____

_____

Reason 3. _____

_____

VOCABULARY
Academic Vocabulary

This reading is intended for an "academic" audience rather than a general one. Therefore, its vocabulary is different from what you might find in a magazine article. Here are some words and phrases that are "academic." Define them below. Can you identify any others? Look up any words you don't understand.

1. *mythic stature* _____

_____

2. *pattern of beliefs* _____

_____

3. *literary conventions* _____

_____

4. *middle-class ethic* _____

_____

THINK ABOUT IT

1. What is your opinion of the author's analysis of Superman?

2. Identify another superhero comic book character. Discuss what that character might symbolize. (Some to look for: Batman, Spiderman, Wonder Woman)

3. The author claims that the idea of being an "immigrant and an orphan" makes Superman particularly American. Why is this so? Are there any other American stories that celebrate being an immigrant or an orphan?

S Y N T H E S I S

Discussion and Debate

1. How do the ideas of dress and icons relate? Do we associate cultural icons with particular styles of dress? Is their dress important to how we think about them?

2. Levis are an "icon" of American culture. Superman and Elvis are icons, too. What other people or things do you think are American icons? List as many as you can think of. Compare your answers with a partner's.

3. Many people become nearly obsessed with certain icons. For example, some people go to the same movie dozens of times, visit Elvis's Graceland home frequently, or collect pictures of Madonna. What is your opinion of this behavior? Are there any icons you are a big fan of?

4. Think of an additional question to ask your classmates about the ideas or opinions presented in this chapter.

Writing Topics

1. Go to a public place and observe how people are dressed. Write an observational report on their clothing. What conclusions can you draw from your observations?

2. Write a letter to a friend in which you explain to him or her something you've learned about America or Americans from this chapter.

3. Write a short essay explaining how dress is similar or different in your country and the United States.

On Your Own

1. Identify someone you think is an American cultural icon. Look at the magazines, the Internet, or other resources to find information on this icon. Discuss your findings with your class.

2. Interview three people about the topics in this chapter. Here are some questions to get you started. Be sure to add some of your own:

   • What is your favorite piece of clothing? Why?

   • Do you think schools should require students to wear uniforms?

   • How much do you think you spend on clothing in one year?

   • Who is the most important American icon, in your opinion?

   • Who is the most famous American, in your opinion?

★★

A L M A N A C   For additional cultural information, refer to the Almanac on pages 221–234. The Almanac contains lists of useful facts, maps, and other information to enhance your learning.

ALMANAC

★★★

1. Map of the United States showing state capitals

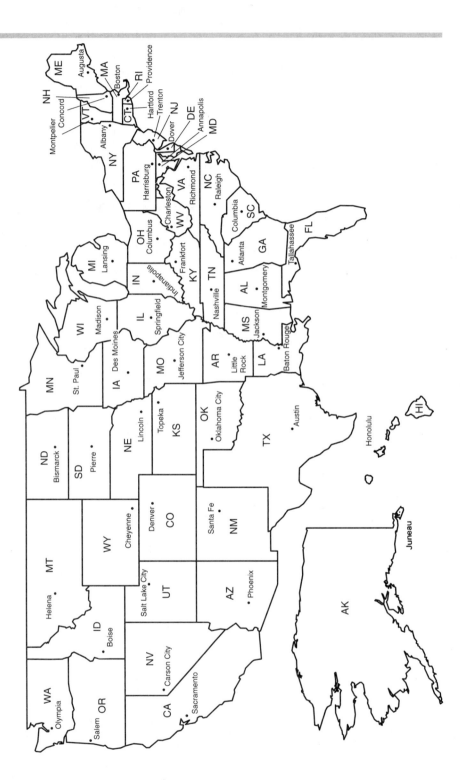

2. Geographic Map of the United States

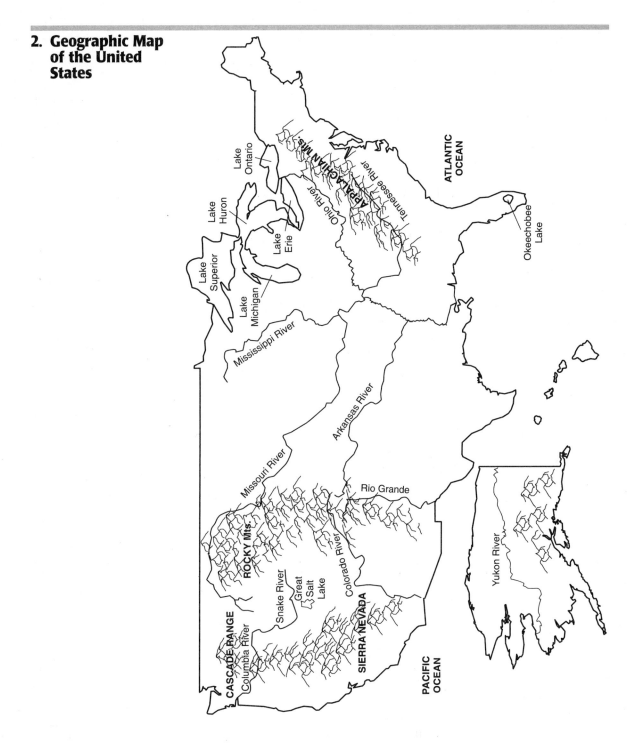

3. Total Population of the States in the United States

	Latest Estimate
UNITED STATES	248,709,873
ALABAMA	4,040,587
ARKANSAS	550,043
ARIZONA	3,665,228
ARKANSAS	2,350,725
CALIFORNIA	29,760,021
COLORADO	3,294,394
CONNECTICUT	3,287,116
DELAWARE	666,168
DISTRICT OF COLUMBIA	606,900
FLORIDA	12,937,926
GEORGIA	6,478,216
HAWAII	1,108,229
IDAHO	1,006,749
ILLINOIS	11,430,602
INDIANA	5,544,159
IOWA	2,776,755
KANSAS	2,477,574
KENTUCKY	3,685,296
LOUISIANA	4,219,973
MAINE	1,227,928
MARYLAND	4,781,468
MASSACHUSETTS	6,016,425
MICHIGAN	9,295,297
MINNESOTA	4,375,099
MISSISSIPPI	2,573,216
MISSOURI	5,117,073
MONTANA	799,065
NEBRASKA	1,578,385
NEVADA	1,201,833
NEW HAMPSHIRE	1,109,252
NEW JERSEY	7,730,188
NEW MEXICO	1,515,069
NEW YORK	17,990,455
NORTH CAROLINA	6,628,637
NORTH DAKOTA	638,800
OHIO	10,847,115
OKLAHOMA	3,145,585
OREGON	2,842,321
PENNSYLVANIA	11,881,643
RHODE ISLAND	1,003,464
SOUTH CAROLINA	3,486,703
SOUTH DAKOTA	696,004
TENNESSEE	4,877,185
TEXAS	16,986,510
UTAH	1,722,850
VERMONT	562,758
VIRGINIA	6,187,358
WASHINGTON	4,866,692
WEST VIRGINIA	1,793,477
WISCONSIN	4,891,769
WYOMING	453,588

Source: Population Estimates Branch, U.S. Bureau of the Census, Release date: Aug. 1996

4. Population of States in the United States by Ethnic Background

	Total	Total Hispanic	White Total	White Hispanic	White non-Hispanic	Black	American Indian	Asian & Pacific Islander
UNITED STATES	265,283,783	28,268,895	219,748,786	25,771,113	193,977,673	33,503,435	2,288,119	9,743,443
ALABAMA	4,273,084	35,857	3,125,926	30,401	3,095,525	1,103,986	15,385	27,787
ALASKA	607,007	22,356	462,255	18,075	444,180	23,325	95,339	26,088
ARIZONA	4,428,068	941,479	3,936,621	880,294	3,056,327	153,888	248,490	89,069
ARKANSAS	2,509,793	40,852	2,076,142	36,088	2,040,054	403,466	13,170	17,015
CALIFORNIA	31,878,234	9,630,188	25,491,661	9,011,827	16,479,834	2,371,293	303,494	3,711,786
COLORADO	3,822,676	535,917	3,535,813	503,635	3,032,178	164,343	35,538	86,982
CONNECTICUT	3,274,238	253,245	2,895,483	223,705	2,671,778	297,984	7,906	72,865
DELAWARE	724,842	22,774	572,853	19,365	553,488	136,062	2,434	13,493
DISTRICT OF CO- LUMBIA	543,213	37,705	184,638	30,035	154,603	340,837	1,692	16,046
FLORIDA	14,399,985	2,022,110	11,930,830	1,879,468	10,051,362	2,172,252	51,592	245,311
GEORGIA	7,353,225	187,392	5,130,880	163,122	4,967,758	2,074,548	17,086	130,711
HAWAII	1,183,723	93,100	395,969	46,444	349,525	35,514	6,515	745,725
IDAHO	1,189,251	80,976	1,154,199	75,050	1,079,149	6,438	15,856	12,758
ILLINOIS	11,846,544	1,136,282	9,639,662	1,063,265	8,576,397	1,806,901	26,210	373,771
INDIANA	5,840,528	129,277	5,297,205	118,023	5,179,182	477,928	14,022	51,373
IOWA	2,851,792	49,865	2,754,355	45,164	2,709,191	55,047	8,358	34,032
KANSAS	2,572,150	124,842	2,355,375	112,989	2,242,386	152,166	22,903	41,706
KENTUCKY	3,883,723	28,543	3,573,069	24,406	3,548,663	279,930	5,891	24,833
LOUISIANA	4,350,579	109,969	2,884,225	94,301	2,789,924	1,393,678	19,346	53,330
MAINE	1,243,316	8,446	1,223,690	7,598	1,216,092	5,729	5,578	8,319
MARYLAND	5,071,604	170,052	3,494,905	141,828	3,353,077	1,373,129	15,343	188,227
MASSACHUSETTS	6,092,352	348,181	5,499,644	275,693	5,223,951	377,715	14,279	200,714
MICHIGAN	9,594,350	242,128	8,024,496	215,033	7,809,463	1,368,804	58,939	142,111
MINNESOTA	4,657,758	76,044	4,360,889	65,814	4,295,075	128,056	56,934	111,879
MISSISSIPPI	2,716,115	20,149	1,702,058	15,988	1,686,070	986,895	9,638	17,524
MISSOURI	5,358,692	76,755	4,685,274	67,767	4,617,507	597,565	20,418	55,435
MONTANA	879,372	14,550	816,791	12,244	804,547	3,216	54,226	5,139
NEBRASKA	1,652,093	63,294	1,552,364	57,640	1,494,724	64,953	14,744	20,032
NEVADA	1,603,163	226,039	1,388,507	205,786	1,182,721	118,440	28,120	68,096
NEW HAMPSHIRE	1,162,481	15,852	1,139,475	14,391	1,125,084	8,066	2,281	12,659
NEW JERSEY	7,987,933	920,085	6,414,926	792,965	5,621,961	1,157,171	20,622	395,214
NEW MEXICO	1,713,407	677,341	1,490,295	649,808	840,487	43,001	157,181	22,930
NEW YORK	18,184,774	2,537,597	13,991,765	1,916,575	12,075,190	3,198,235	72,963	921,811
NORTH CARO- LINA	7,322,870	134,384	5,518,807	114,871	5,403,936	1,624,259	93,963	85,841
NORTH DAKOTA	643,539	6,359	604,844	5,326	599,518	4,111	29,392	5,192
OHIO	11,172,782	168,711	9,766,839	149,373	9,617,466	1,264,493	22,356	119,094
OKLAHOMA	3,300,902	114,823	2,745,517	95,578	2,649,939	253,319	260,501	41,565
OREGON	3,203,735	177,233	3,005,721	162,308	2,843,413	57,752	44,116	96,146
PENNSYLVANIA	12,056,112	292,050	10,690,370	245,200	10,445,170	1,162,462	17,067	186,213
RHODE ISLAND	990,225	59,475	917,164	47,509	869,655	47,050	4,683	21,328
SOUTH CARO- LINA	3,698,746	40,771	2,543,890	33,747	2,510,143	1,115,869	8,754	30,233
SOUTH DAKOTA	732,405	7,266	666,157	5,782	660,375	4,542	57,221	4,485
TENNESSEE	5,319,654	52,302	4,385,464	44,667	4,340,796	874,592	11,843	47,756
TEXAS	19,128,261	5,503,372	16,203,786	5,309,635	10,894,151	2,336,165	90,035	498,275
UTAH	2,000,494	121,641	1,907,846	112,675	1,795,171	16,747	28,472	47,429
VERMONT	588,654	5,704	578,103	5,195	572,908	3,500	1,695	5,356
VIRGINIA	6,675,451	223,828	5,111,445	195,348	4,916,097	1,322,722	17,780	223,504
WASHINGTON	5,532,939	321,684	4,944,646	284,864	4,659,782	189,241	99,369	299,683
WEST VIRGINIA	1,825,754	9,892	1,756,915	8,790	1,748,125	57,600	2,544	8,695
WISCONSIN	5,159,795	122,622	4,756,004	109,880	4,646,124	284,368	45,277	74,146
WYOMING	481,400	27,536	463,029	25,578	437,451	4,082	10,558	3,731

Note: In the categories given above, American Indian includes Eskimo and Aleut

Source: Administrative Records and Methodology Research Branch—U.S. Bureau of the Census

5. Major Events in United States History

1700
1754 — French and Indian War
Boston Tea Party — 1773
1776 — Declaration of Independence
Slavery is illegal in Massachusetts — 1783
1789 — George Washington becomes President
Building of the White House starts — 1792

1800 — Federal government moves to Washington, D.C.
War of 1812 — 1812
1845 — Texas becomes a state
Gold discovered in California — 1848
1861 — Civil War begins
Lincoln frees the slaves — 1863
1865 — Civil War ends

1900
San Francisco earthquake — 1906
1917 — World War I begins
Word War II begins — 1941
1955 — Supreme Court orders school integration
President John F. Kennedy is killed — 1963
1968 — Martin Luther King, Jr. is killed
200th Anniversary of U.S. independence — 1976
1995 — Oklahoma City terrorist bombing

6. Weights and Measures, Temperatures (Celsius and Fahrenheit)

Weights and Measures

1 pound (lb.) = 453.6 grams (g.)
16 ounces (oz.) = 1 pound (lb.)
2,000 pounds (lb.) = 1 ton

1 inch (in. or ″) = 2.54 centimeters (cm)
1 foot (ft or ′) = 0.3048 meters (m)
12 inches (12″) = 1 foot (1′)
3 feet (3′) = 1 yard (yd.)
1 mile = 5,280 feet (5,280′)

Temperature chart: Celsius and Fahrenheight

degrees (°) Celsius (C) = ⅝ degrees Fahrenheight) − 32

degrees (°) Fahrenheight (C) = ⅝ degrees Celsius) + 32

C:	100°	30°	25°	20°	15°	10°	5°	0°	−5°
F:	212°	86°	77°	68°	59°	50°	41°	32°	23°

7. Immigration Patterns 1820 to Present

Countries	1820–1996	1981–90	1971–80	1961–70	1951–60	1941–50	1820–1940
Europe:							
Albania	12,230	479	329	98	59	85	2,040
Austria	2,664,728	4,636	9,478	20,621	67,106	24,860	2,534,617
Belgium	212,894	5,706	5,329	9,192	18,575	12,189	158,205
Bulgaria	78,029	2,342	1,188	619	104	375	65,856
Former Czechoslovakia	156,848	11,500	6,023	3,273	918	8,347	120,013
Denmark	374,287	5,380	4,439	9,201	10,984	5,393	335,025
Estonia	2,254	137	91	163	185	212	506
Finland	40,315	3,265	2,868	4,192	4,925	2,503	19,593
France	795,259	23,124	25,069	45,237	51,121	38,809	594,998
Germany	7,105,301	70,111	74,414	190,796	477,765	226,578	6,021,951
Greece	704,679	29,130	92,369	85,969	47,608	8,973	430,608
Hungary	167,871	9,764	6,550	5,401	36,637	3,469	1,609,158
Ireland	4,780,891	32,823	11,490	32,966	48,362	14,789	4,580,557
Italy	5,353,213	32,894	129,368	214,111	185,491	57,661	4,719,223
Latvia	6,603	359	207	510	352	361	1,192
Lithuania	7,967	482	248	562	242	683	2,201
Luxembourg	3,284	234	307	556	684	820	565
Netherlands	382,109	11,958	10,492	30,606	52,277	14,860	253,759
Norway	756,448	3,901	3,941	15,484	22,935	10,100	697,095
Poland	743,376	97,390	37,234	53,539	9,985	7,571	414,755
Portugal	518,753	40,020	101,710	76,065	19,588	7,423	256,044
Romania	246,657	39,963	12,393	2,531	1,039	1,076	156,945
Spain	289,611	15,698	39,141	44,659	7,894	2,898	170,123
Sweden	1,398,578	10,211	6,531	17,116	21,697	10,665	1,325,208
Switzerland	362,792	7,076	8,235	18,453	17,675	10,547	295,680
United Kingdom	5,197,150	142,123	137,374	213,822	202,824	139,306	4,266,561
Former U.S.S.R.	3,749,777	84,081	38,961	2,465	671	571	3,343,361
Former Yugoslavia	158,540	19,182	30,540	20,381	8,225	1,576	56,787
Other Europe	65,875	2,661	4,049	4,904	9,799	3,447	36,060
Total Europe	36,410,452	705,630	800,368	1,123,492	1,325,727	621,147	32,468,776
Asia/Middle East:							
China	1,232,740	388,686	124,326	34,764	9,657	16,709	382,173
India	703,339	261,841	164,134	27,189	1,973	1,761	9,873
Israel	152,473	36,353	37,713	29,602	25,476	476	—
Japan	498,333	43,248	49,775	39,988	46,250	1,555	277,591
Turkey	425,601	20,843	13,399	10,142	3,519	798	361,236
Other Asia	5,010,282	2,042,025	1,198,831	285,957	66,374	15,729	44,053
Total Asia	8,000,844	2,066,455	1,588,178	427,642	153,249	37,028	1,074,926
America:							
Canada and Newfoundland	4,348,541	119,204	169,939	413,310	377,952	171,718	3,005,728
Central America	1,153,217	458,753	134,640	101,330	44,751	21,665	49,154
Mexico	5,246,392	1,653,250	640,294	453,937	299,811	60,589	778,255
South America	1,588,408	455,977	295,741	257,954	91,628	21,831	121,302
West Indies	3,372,716	892,392	741,126	470,213	123,091	49,725	446,971
Other America	117,574	1,352	995	19,630	59,711	29,276	56
Total America	15,945,081	3,580,928	1,982,735	1,716,374	996,944	354,804	4,401,466
Africa	561,569	192,212	80,779	28,954	14,092	7,367	26,060

Countries	1820–1996	1981–90	1971–80	1961–70	1951–60	1941–50	1820–1940
Australia and New Zealand	160,870	20,169	23,788	19,562	11,506	13,805	54,437
Pacific Islands	63,034	21,041	17,454	5,560	1,470	746	11,089
Countries not specified	272,254	196	12	93	12,491	142	253,689
Total all countries	61,207,884	7,338,062	4,493,314	3,321,677	2,515,479	1,035,039	38,290,443

Source: Department of Justice, Immigration and Naturalization Service.

8. Top Ten Holiday Movies and Foods

Top 10 Christmas Holiday Movies

1. "The Santa Clause"
2. "It's a Wonderful Life"
3. "A Christmas Story"
4. "White Christmas"
5. "Miracle on 34th Street"
6. "Home Alone"
7. "Frosty the Snowman"
8. "Nightmare Before Christmas"
9. "Mickey's Christmas Carol"
10. "National Lampoon's Christmas Vacation"

Top 10 Christmas Holiday Foods

1. Cookies
2. Turkey
3. Eggnog
4. Candy Canes
5. Chips and Dip
6. Gingerbread Men
7. Stuffing
8. Deviled Eggs
9. Honey Baked Ham
10. Popcorn Balls

Compiled by Amy Au, *Spokesman Online*, http://whs.dist214.k12.il.us/spokesman/121595/ttfhi.html

9. U.S. Legal or Public Holidays

DATE	HOLIDAY	BACKGROUND
January 1	New Year's Day	first day of the year according to the western calendar
Third Monday in January	Martin Luther King, Jr. Day	honors the late civil rights leader; became a holiday in 1986
February 12	Lincoln's Birthday*	honors the 16th President of the United States
February 22	Washington's Birthday*	honors the first President of the United States
Last Monday in May	Memorial Day	originally honored those who died in the Civil War; now honors all who have died in U.S. wars
July 4	Independence Day	celebrates the adoption of the U.S. Declaration of Independence in 1776
First Monday in September	Labor Day	honors workers; first celebrated in 1882
October 12	Columbus Day	commemorates the discovery of America by Christopher Columbus in 1492
November 11	Veteran's Day	originally celebrated the end of World War I; now honors all men and women who have served in the U.S. armed forces
Fourth Thursday in November	Thanksgiving Day	a day of thanks for food and other blessings; first celebrated in the U.S. at Plymouth Colony in 1621
December 25	Christmas Day	anniversary of the birth of Jesus Christ

*In most places, these two holidays are celebrated together on a single day called President's Day, which falls on the third Monday in February.

10. Slogans of the 50 States

Alabama
Motto: Audemus jura nostra defendere [We Dare Defend Our Rights]
Nickname: Heart of Dixie / Cotton State / Camellia State

Alaska
Motto: North To The Future
Nickname: Last Frontier / Great Land / Land of the Midnight Sun

Arizona
Motto: Ditat Deus [God enriches]
Nickname: Grand Canyon State

Arkansas
Motto: Regnat populus [The people rule]
Nickname: The Natural State / Land of Opportunity / Wonder State

California
Motto: Eureka [I have found it]
Nickname: Golden State

Colorado
Motto: Nil sine Numine [Nothing without Providence]
Nickname: Centennial State

Connecticut
Motto: Qui transtulit sustinet [He who transplanted still sustains]
Nickname: Constitution State / Provision State / Nutmeg State

Delaware
Motto: Liberty and Independence
Nickname: First State / Diamond State

Florida
Motto: In God We Trust
Nickname: Sunshine State / Peninsula State

Georgia
Motto: Wisdom, justice, and moderation
Nickname: Peach State / Goober state/ Empire State of the South

Hawaii
Motto: Ua mau ke ea o ka aina I ka pono [The life of the land is perpetuated in righteousness]
Nickname: Aloha State / Paradise of the Pacific

Idaho
Motto: Esto perpetua (Let it be perpetual) [It is forever]
Nickname: Gem State

Illinois
Motto: State sovereignty, national union
Nickname: Land of Lincoln / Prairie State

Indiana
Motto: The crossroads of America
Nickname: Hoosier State

Iowa
Motto: Our liberties we prize and our rights we will maintain
Nickname: Hawkeye State / Corn State

Kansas
Motto: Ad astra per aspera [To the stars through difficulties]
Nickname: Sunflower State

Kentucky
Motto: United we stand, devided we fall
Nickname: Bluegrass State

Louisiana
Motto: Union, justice, and confidence
Nickname: Pelican State

Maine
Motto: Dirigo [I direct]
Nickname: Pine Tree State

Maryland
Motto: Fatti maschil parole femine [Manly deeds womanly words]
Nickname: Old Line State / Free State

Massachusetts
Motto: Ense petit placidam sub libertate quietem [By the sword we seek peace, but peace only under liberty]
Nickname: Bay State / Old Colony

Michigan
Motto: Si quaeris peninsulam amoenam, circumspice [If you seek a pleasent peninsula, look about you.]
Nickname: Great Lakes State/ Wolverine State / Water Wonderland

Minnesota
  Motto: L'Etoile du nord [The star of the
    north]
  Nickname: North Star State / Gopher State /
    Bread and Butter State
Mississippi
  Motto: Virtute et armis [By valor and arms]
  Nickname: Magnolia State
Missouri
  Motto: Salus pouli suprema lex esto [The
    welfare of the people shall be the supreme
    law]
  Nickname: Show Me State
Montana
  Motto: Oro y plata [Gold and Silver]
  Nickname: Treasure State
Nebraska
  Motto: Equality before the law
  Nickname: Cornhusker State
Nevada
  Motto: All for our country
  Nickname: The Silver State / Sagebrush
    State / Battle Born State
New Hampshire
  Motto: Live free or die
  Nickname: Granite State
New Jersey
  Motto: Liberty and Prosperity
  Nickname: Garden State
New Mexico
  Motto: Crescit eundo [It grows as it goes]
  Nickname: Land of Enchantment
New York
  Motto: Excelsior
  Nickname: Empire State / Excelsior State
North Carolina
  Motto: Esse quam videri [To be, rather than
    to seem]
  Nickname: Tar Heel State / Old North State
North Dakota
  Motto: Liberty and union, now and forever,
    one and [inseparable]
  Nickname: Peace Garden State / Flickertail
    State / Sioux State

Ohio
  Motto: With God, all things are possible
  Nickname: Buckeye State
Oklahoma
  Motto: Labor omnia vincit [Labor conquers all
    things]
  Nickname: Sooner State
Oregon
  Motto: Alis Volat Propiis [She Flies With Her
    Own Wings]
  Nickname: Beaver State
Pennsylvania
  Motto: Virtue, Liberty, and Independence
  Nickname: Keystone State
Rhode Island
  Motto: Hope
  Nickname: The Ocean State / Little Rhody
South Carolina
  Mottoes: Animis opibusque parati / Dum spiro
    spero [Prepared in mind and resources /
    While I breathe, I hope]
  Nickname: Palmetto State
South Dakota
  Motto: Under God the people rule
  Nickname: Mt. Rushmore State / Coyote State
Tennessee
  Motto: Agriculture and commerce
  Nickname: Volunteer State
Texas
  Motto: Friendship
  Nickname: Lone Star State
Utah
  Motto: Industry
  Nickname: Beehive State
Vermont
  Motto: Freedom and unity
  Nickname: Green Mountain State
Virginia
  Motto: Sic semper tyrannis [Thus always to
    tyrants]
  Nickname: Old Dominion
Washington
  Motto: Alki [Bye and Bye]
  Nickname: Evergreen State

West Virginia
  Motto: Montani semper liberi
  Nickname: Mountain State
Wisconsin
  Motto: Forward
  Nickname: Badger State

Wyoming
  Motto: Equal rights
  Nicknames: Equality State
District of Columbia
  Motto: Justitia Omnibus (Justice to all)

11. Popular Sports Movies

Tin Cup (1996), golf
When We Were Kings (1996), boxing
Jerry Maguire (1996), football
Forrest Gump (1994), running and football
A League of Their Own (1992), baseball
Field of Dreams (1989),baseball
Bull Durham (1988), baseball
The Natural (1984), baseball
Chariots of Fire (1981), running
Raging Bull (1980), boxing
North Dallas Forty (1979), football
Rocky (1976), boxing
Bang the Drum Slowly (1973), baseball
Brian's Song (1972), football
On the Waterfront (1954), boxing

12. Irregular Past Tenses and Past Participles

Simple Form	Past	Past Participle
be	was, were	been
become	became	become
begin	began	begun
bite	bit	bitten
blow	blew	blown
break	broke	broken
bring	brought	brought
buy	bought	bought
cost	cost	cost
do	did	done
drink	drank	drunk
drive	drove	driven
feel	felt	felt
fit	fit	fit
fly	flew	flown
get	got	gotten
give	gave	given
go	went	gone
have	had	had
hide	hid	hidden
hit	hit	hit
know	knew	known
lay	laid	laid
let	let	let
lie (down)	lay	lain
lie (untruth)	lied	lied
pay	paid	paid
read	read	read
ride	rode	ridden
shut	shut	shut
steal	stole	stolen
take	took	taken
teach	taught	taught
wake	woke	woken
wear	wore	worn

13. Common Prefixes and Suffixes

Common Prefixes

Prefix	Meaning	Example
after-	after	aftertaste
ambi-	both	ambidextrous
anti-	against	antiwar
aqua-	water	aquarium
audi-	sound	auditorium
auto-	self	autobiography
bi-	two	bilingual
co-	with	cooperate
dis-	negative of	disappear
ex-	in the past	ex-wife
hemi-	half	hemisphere
im-	not	immature
inter-	between, among	international
intra-	within	intrastate
micro-	small	microscope
multi-	many	multiracial
non-	not	nonsense
post-	after	postwar
re-	again	remember
un-	not	unusual
zoo-	animal	zoology

Common Suffixes

Suffix	Meaning	Example
-an	belonging to	American
-arium	place, building	aquarium
-chrome	color	monochrome
-en	consisting of	wooden
-er	person who does an action	writer
-ese	relating to	Japanese
-est	most	biggest
-gram	written	telegram
-graph	written	autograph
-ion	process	communication
-meter	measuring device	speedometer
-ness	quality	rudeness
-phone	sound	telephone
-sphere	globelike	hemisphere
-ster	one who is	youngster
-ward	direction	backward
-wide	extent	worldwide